The Red Hills
of Essex

Studying Salt
in England

D1452299

Ian W. Brown

2013

The Red Hills of Essex: Studying Salt in England

ISBN 978-0-9883893-4-2

Borgo Publishing
3811 Derby Downs Drive
Tuscaloosa, Alabama 35405
www.borgopublishing.com

Book cover and text design by
Easty Lambert-Brown, Borgo Publishing

John Constable. The Hay Wain, 1821.
Oil on canvas, 130.2 x 185.4 cm.
Presented by Henry Vaughan, 1886 (NG1207).
National Gallery, London, Great Britain

Cover photo image by Maleah Tidmore, Birmingham, Alabama.
Email: maleahtidmore@aol.com

Printed in the USA

Dedicated to Charles Dickens and Rudyard Kipling
Celebrated Authors of *American Notes*
among other things

There are many passages in this book, where I have been at some pains to resist the temptation of troubling my readers with my own deductions and conclusions: preferring that they should judge for themselves, from such premises as I have laid before them. My only object in the outset, was, to carry them with me faithfully wheresoever I went: and that task I have discharged.
—Charles Dickens, *American Notes*

If ever you meet an American, be good to him.
—Rudyard Kipling, *American Notes*

Contents

Figures

Preface

The Red Hills of the Essex coast in England are monuments to a vanished industry that extracted salt from seawater. It was an industry that can be traced back to the last centuries B.C. and which continued to thrive when Britain became part of the Roman Empire in A.D. 43. The hills themselves were low mounds of red earth, barely a few metres high. Their excavation has brought to light a treasury of the fired-clay equipment known as briquetage that was used for evaporating brine to produce sea salt. Farming has levelled most of the Red Hills now, but they can still be glimpsed in a freshly ploughed field as expanses of red earth standing out against the dark brown soil. They are well worth a visit. As the plates in this book demonstrate so graphically, they are to be found in some of the most evocative and beautiful stretches of the Essex coastline.

My work at Colchester Museum often involves making the archaeological collections available to students and scholars. Most come from universities and colleges in Britain, but every year or so we have a visit from a scholar based overseas. It gives us an opportunity to discuss archaeology with those in the know and to keep abreast of current research. In fact, such work is one of the joys of my profession. But I have to confess to astonishment when I was approached by a Professor Brown from far away in the U.S. state of Alabama with a request to see our Red Hills material. And what a remarkable and useful visit it turned out to be. Ian had the advantage over us in Essex of having studied salt making on a global basis. It never occurred to me that I would ever see a published paper comparing our own Essex finds with material from China, but Ian did it. We all learnt so much from his visit; and we now have this lovely book before us, one of the most important statements on the subject since the magisterial 1990 survey by the Colchester Archaeological Group. It is always a delight when a research visit from a scholar culminates in a significant published contribution to the subject. We could never have done it, and it is ironic to reflect that one of our leading experts on the Red Hills of Essex nowadays is the Professor of Anthropology at the University of Alabama.

But this book is more than an archaeological treatise. Remarkably, it combines the archaeology with a travelogue that gives Britons like myself a rare opportunity to see ourselves as others see us. Maybe Ian was disposed to like us anyway, but I think we come out of it well. It only goes to show how museum visits by scholars from overseas are a force for international understanding and friendship as well as archaeological science. Thank you, Ian.

Dr. Paul R. Sealey, F.S.A.
Curator of Archaeology
Colchester Museum

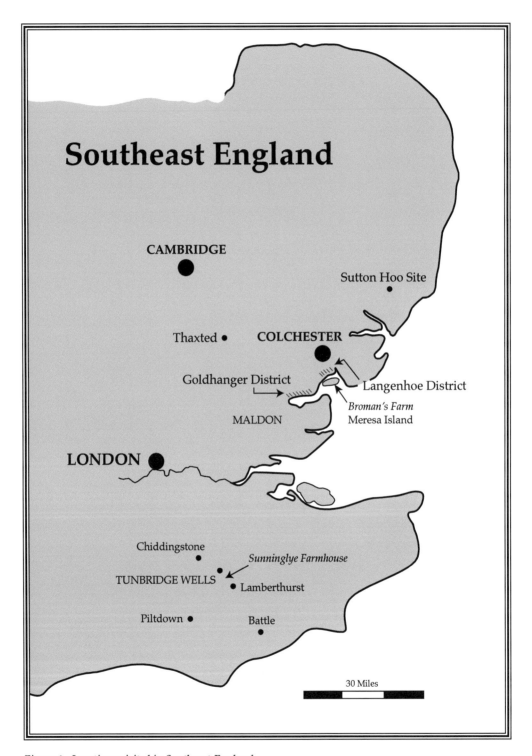

Figure 1. Locations visited in Southeast England.

Introduction

The one unique thing about the Blount Undergraduate Initiative at the University of Alabama is that it permits one to teach seminar courses that do not fit the mold. Although I have been studying salt for well over a quarter of a century, it was not until 2005 that I had the opportunity to teach a course on the subject. The official title of the course is "Salt of the Earth, an Anthropological Perspective" and it deals with the role of salt in the growth and development of civilizations throughout the world. One of my favorite case studies is the famous "Red Hills of Essex." Dotting the coastline of southeast England, especially in the districts south of Colchester (Figure 1), are hundreds of heaps of red soil, rich in crude baked clay objects. They have been recognized as strange features on the landscape for decades, if not centuries, but it was not until the turn of the twentieth century that they entered the world of the scientist. In 1906 the Red Hills Exploration Committee was formed in Essex, comprised of a multitude of scholars from many different disciplines. Their one main goal was to discover the purpose(s) of these enigmatic Red Hills. Because of the coastal positioning of these hills, they suspected that salt production was the prime reason for their existence, but even after years of diligent research, they still were unable to solve the riddle of just how production might have occurred.

Years ago, when I was composing my book on *Salt and the Eastern North American Indian*,[1] I looked to the investigations of the Red Hills Exploration Committee for comparative information. I especially drew from the 1970s investigations of Kay De Brisay of the Colchester Archaeological Group, a group of scholars who made (and continue to make) many significant contributions to understanding the operation of these ancient salt works. Now that several Red Hills have been excavated over the past four decades, we not only have

---

[1] Brown 1980.

good descriptive information on the artifacts, but there is a wealth of knowledge that has accumulated on the features with which they are unquestionably associated. The trouble is that the Red Hills are the debris from the production, so that the artifacts themselves are seldom found in association with features, and that's what makes the riddle so difficult to solve. The ancient salt producers of the Late Iron Age and Early Roman period provided no written records as to their activities, but fortunately they did leave clues in the ground. One would think that thousands of objects combined with a few dozen excavated hearths and pits, really should be more than enough to come to terms with this industry, but sadly that is not the case. The process still continues to elude us. The information is certainly there, but as so often happens in archaeology, it is fragmentary and frustrating.

The more I read about the Red Hills of Essex in preparing for my class, the more intrigued I became. I had written and talked about briquetage[2] in articles and conference papers for many years, but I had never actually seen any of it from Europe, where it was defined. How could I be so certain as to what it was and how it functioned without having ever actually handled the equipment? Ironically, I had seen more briquetage in China than I had the Western World,[3] so clearly it was time to expand my studies. What finally convinced me of this necessity were the detailed maps of the Essex coastline included in the various articles by Francis W. Reader in 1908 and 1910. In these works he not only described the excavations and artifacts, but excellent maps showed just how a traveler could get to the sites. Here was an opportunity for me to acquaint myself with the landscape upon which these early salt producers labored. I felt that if I could just see the area I would have a far better appreciation of the industry, and if I could also get into some of the museums, then perhaps I could gain access to the collections. I fully recognized that I would be unable to contribute much in what could only be a short visit, but for nothing else I would learn from the experience and be able to talk far more intelligently about the subject with my students.

Thus was born my own personal "Essex Red Hills Project." During the winter and spring of 2005 I made arrangements to spend two weeks in southeast England in late May. My project was financed by travel and research funds from non-salary earnings in the Blount program as well as a generous award of $1,500 that came annually as part of my three-year term as a College of Arts

---

[2]   Briquetage is a French term for baked clay objects that result from the making of salt.

[3]   Brown 1999a-b, Falkenhausen and Brown 2006.

and Sciences Distinguished Teaching Fellow. Because of car rental agencies unique ability to charge double their original estimates, however, a significant amount of personal investment also was involved. The whole project cost on the order of $3,700.

I am particularly grateful for having been admitted to see the wonderful collections of the Colchester Museum. Dr. Paul R. Sealey, Curator of Archaeology, donated two days of his precious time to help me in my studies, for which I am most grateful. I cannot say enough as to how important it is to be inundated with artifactual evidence. Even when one enters a region as a novice, the experience is most useful. Upon examining twenty-six boxes of briquetage, however, I realized that I had far more questions than before. I also recognized that some of what I had read before did not match the data in important ways.

What I offer here is the story of my education on the mysterious Red Hills, and I present it as the story unfolds. This may be a bit frustrating for the student of salt who may just wish "the facts", but facts quite simply do not exist without context. Facts appear only insofar as the researcher recognizes them, and their importance grows through time or diminishes. I know all of this sounds very Post-Modern, but I firmly believe that facts and how they relate to each other are dependent upon how a researcher's thoughts come together. What I mean by this is that although artifacts, features, and whatever limited associations are already "out there", so to speak, to be grabbed by whoever passes by who bears an interest in ancient salt production, they do not just jell in some miraculous way into a masterful understanding of process. How they come together in the mind of the scholar depends on his or her experiences. Consequently, the ways in which archaeological thought crystallize is perhaps as important in the long run as conclusions. The latter always do seem to change as new data appear (as they should), but any one scholar's journey in trying to come to terms with a riddle of the past, no matter what that riddle might be, is perhaps of greater interest to later generations. It is because of this that the reader, if he or she is willing, must first be subjected to my "daily log."

What follows are my journal entries for two weeks of study as I explored the mystery of the Essex Red Hills. I also had some breaks from salt, as one cannot go to England without visiting castles, abbeys, barrows, and pubs. My thoughts are offered on these and many other subjects in the pages ahead. The less tolerant reader, however, may just wish to leave the life of Ian Brown and turn to Part III (see page 115) to see my analysis and proposed solution to the riddle of salt making in Essex. I say solution, but rest assured that nothing is ever solved or final. What I offer is a model that I believe fits well with the data. This model was first introduced in my article, "Comparison of the Briquetage from Zhongba to Finds from the Essex Red Hills of Southeast England" (Brown 2010). However, as that volume was published in China and has not been widely distributed, I imagine that much of what is said here is new to those who are interested in how salt manufacture might have occurred in southeast England. It is important to note, however, that this model is in dire need of testing. I don't believe any archaeologist has ever finished a project with the words, "No more needs to be done," and I shall not do so here.

Although I basically offer the journal entries verbatim, there are some changes in the text. For example, I doubt that the reader either needs or cares to know what time I went to bed or when I woke up each and every day. I myself don't really understand why I record such inane facts, but I do. To ease the flow of the text, I have removed many (perhaps not enough) of the offending passages. Also, because I compose my journals by pen, horrors upon horrors I sometimes make spelling and grammatical mistakes. That can be excused in script perhaps, but not here, so hopefully I have corrected all such errors. And because I am not always as nice as I wish to be in my journals I have made some alterations for fear of offending people who may not understand my subtle wit, or the lack thereof.

The beauty of typing up journal entries so soon after events occur, which is what I generally do, is that embellishments can be made with a degree of reliability. The journal is a "morning after" snapshot of the daily happenings, but sometimes the impacts of events are not felt until several days later. As a result, in those cases wherein I felt I had more to say on the matter, I have not hesitated to add such musings to my journal entries.

I would be remiss not to mention two people who have contributed mightily to the production of this volume. Jessie Foster, a former Blount student at the University of Alabama, is responsible for four artistic renderings of my Essex Red Hills salt making model. And Easty Lambert-Brown, designer and owner of Borgo Publishing and my spouse of many a year, took all of my writings and images and produced, as usual, a most attractive volume on the subject of salt. Whether or not the substance is palatable to the taste shall be left to the reader to decide.

PART I
English Notes, The Journey

Getting to Sunninglye Farmhouse

The date is Monday, May 16. I am in England, safely nestled at Sunninglye Farmhouse near Tunbridge Wells, Kent. As with all forms of travel, or travail, there is work involved. It was not easy, but I got here.

Nancy[4] drove me to Atlanta on Sunday afternoon. Our goodbye was a bit abrupt as they are doing repairs at the Terminal and there was no place to stop and hug. It was a rat race inside as renovation is occurring there too. It was a job finding the end of the International travel line on the Delta ticket window and once I did, I discovered to my chagrin that it stretched halfway around the airport. Panic was starting to set in until I realized that the line was constantly moving and agents were going around collecting people whose flight times were imminent. There were lots of foreign teenagers flying, which was part of the reason for the long delays. And, like most young folk, they are kind of oblivious to the concerns of others.

Once on the plane, things settled down. We got off when they said we would and we arrived within a minute of the established time. En route I started reading *Travels with a Donkey in the Cevannes* by Robert Louis Stevenson and made it through a third of the volume before retiring. I can't sleep on airplanes because of all the noise and activity, but once I put on my night-shades and plug my ears with plastic gel I can pretty well tune myself out. I took off my shoes and planted my left foot beneath my bag so that it would not be rolled on,[5] and then tried to sleep. I should learn, however, to bring some sort of inflatable neck brace, because I always end up with a crick in my neck.

We landed at Gatwick airport south of London at 7 A.M., so I had a full day of jet lag before me. Everything went fine in Customs, but I had a bit of a shock at the Hertz rental when I found out how much insurance was in addition to the car cost. I tried to find out if I was already covered (I seem to remember going through this before), but I couldn't get through to anyone, as it was so early in the States. Thus, I ended up taking "the basic" and did a big gulp.

It's never easy the first day of driving in a new country, and this is especially so in England because of being on the left side of the road. Nevertheless, I bit my lip, pressed the clutch, and jumped out on to the highway in my ordeal by fire. Naturally I ended up going the wrong way, which took me on an

---

[4] My wife now goes by the name Easty, a family name, but in 2005 it was still Nancy and that is how I recorded her in my journal.
[5] My foot that is.

unanticipated adventure. Instead of going due east on A264 toward Tunbridge Wells, I headed north toward Reigate/Redhill. Once that error was discovered I had clearly headed too far out of my way to turn back (sounds like a bad poker game), so I continued going north until I got to the A25 and then set out east. That was all well and good, and I knew I was doing right once I hit the A21, a "dual carriageway" they call it. I set on south to my destination, but failed to take direction well and ended up getting off at the Pembury exit, instead of "just after Pembury," as indicated in my instructions. That was okay, I guess, as I didn't want to get to the B&B too early. I parked my car in a historic section of Tunbridge Wells near a spring that had been discovered in the early 1600s and then had lunch at a pub. I wanted something light, but I don't believe they understand the concept. I had a prawn sandwich on very nice white bread, as well as chips (fries) and a cup of tea. There were a lot of bookstores in this section and I certainly would have taken the time to browse more if I wasn't so worried about just how to get out of Tunbridge Wells. The barkeeper gave me some good advice though and got me back on A264 headed towards the A21. But how was I to go south on it? That I couldn't figure out, so I figured I would go north, get off at the next exchange, do a roundabout (rotary) and head south once more. Would that it would be so easy. It was miles before I even got to an exchange, the exit to Sevenoaks, and I discovered to my chagrin that there was no way to get back on to the A21. Thus, I ended up going all the way north to the A25 and then west to Chipstead, where I had been a couple of hours earlier! Only then could I go south on the A21 once more. It's a good thing I have unlimited mileage on this vehicle.

This time I continued past Pembury and actually did come to a roundabout that had Frant Station as one of its outlets. I took it and headed down a long winding road that was really quite exciting because of its narrowness. As cars approached me at breakneck speed, I felt like a "Knight of old" involved in a jousting match. I just had to keep saying to myself, "To the left, to the left."

I pulled in to Sunninglye Farmhouse (Figure 2) at around 1 p.m. John Petrie, the proprietor, was in the middle of his meal and clearly was not expecting me until later. He was not put out though and seemed happy to meet me and show me about. He has the same face and expressions as Jim Yarbrough, a former Dean of the College of A&S who brought me to Alabama. Thus, I took to him right away. The farmhouse is quite lovely. It is over 500 years old, the core of it at least, and was added on to over the centuries. The oldest parts are the dining room, the adjacent study, and my bedroom, which is immediately above the dining room. Five centuries ago my room would not have been there, as the

Figure 2. The Sunninglye Farmhouse B&B located in Tunbridge Wells, East Sussex.

now dining room area would have been open to the roof. It is not known when they added the floor. The wooden floor in my room dips steeply to the fireplace behind the bedstead. In fact, the head of the bed is set right within the fireplace! A heavy timber framing makes up the roof, which is over six feet tall at its deepest, the fireplace end, and about 5' 8" or so at the opposite wall. One has the impression of being at an amusement park in entering the room. The walls are plastered with a covering of white wash. I have my own private bath, which is nice, but because I am the only guest it would not have made a difference anyways.

I took a nap for a couple of hours. I know that is not the right thing to do to cure jet lag, but I really did need it. Then I went downstairs for a cup of tea, at which time I met Susie, the lady of the house. She is working on her Ph.D. on Kentish history, and had just returned from Canterbury where she was doing some work at the University. She is very nice too. Susie gave me some background on the house and area (Weald for example stands for Wild, and this area is still heavily forested). As we were sitting in the kitchen it started to rain, a nice gentle sprinkling, which was desperately needed they told me. To me everything looks so green and lush that I could not see the necessity, but they know best. Sunninglye is in the Lovely Gardens book of Alastair Sawday's *Special Places to Stay*,[6] and I can clearly see why. Their garden is indeed beautiful.

Figure 3. Many of the buildings in this portion of East Sussex are very old. This structure, which occurs on the lane leading to Sunninglye Farmhouse, is called an Oast barn. It was used for drying hops as part of the brewing process.

John gave me directions to several pubs, and I decided to attend "The Georges" in Frant Station. I had a choice between a pub meal and a full dinner, so I selected the former, the Georges Ploughman Special. This turned out to be an excellent choice as it consisted of a salad, several chunks of Stilton cheese, butter, and warm bread. It hit the spot, as I really did not feel like eating too much. I had a half pint of Bottingers beer with it, which was less than what I wanted, but seeing I was driving a distance, and in the rain, it probably was more than enough. I managed to embarrass myself by almost leaving a tip of 3 bob on a 7 bob meal, and I'm sure the barkeeper and the other gentlemen had a good laugh about that after I left. I explained that I was "new in the country," but the explanation really wasn't necessary.

I got back to the farmhouse with but one wrong turn and nestled in for the evening (Figure 3). I made myself a nice cup of tea, read the *Kent Archaeological Society Newsletter* that Susie gave me, and took some notes on it in my field-

---

[6] I continue to make heavy use of the Alastair Sawday's series in my travels to England, particularly the British Bed & Breakfast volume (King 1999).

book. At about 9:30 or 10:00 P.M., after a wonderful hot bath, very hot, I entered the fine comfort of my bed, with equally comfortable pillows, and I felt the God of Morph take me away to green pastures.

Lamberhurst, a Village on the Weald

It turns out that Sunninglye Farmhouse is on the extreme eastern border of Sussex, despite the fact that Tunbridge Wells is in Kent and their postbox is Kent. I certainly feel as if I am in Kent.

On Tuesday I had a lovely traditional breakfast of two eggs, ham, fried tomatoes, bread, butter, and homemade marmalade. And I started it off with stewed rhubarb, straight from the garden. It was still cold and cloudy, a good day to stay inside, rest, and catch up on all the reading that I had to do with regard to Essex salt. When I meet up with Paul R. Sealey on Thursday I want to be halfway intelligent on the subject. Plus, I was still tired and needed an hour's rest in the afternoon, despite doing nothing that required energy.

I walked all around the grounds in the late morning just for a break from my readings. They do not have a lot of acreage to tramp around on, but I did enjoy the gardens, both flower and vegetable, and I even took a stroll in the fields to pay my respects to the horses, Smoky and Folly. Smoky expected a feed, and when he realized he was not to get one, he showed me his backside and farted. Fortunately I was upwind. At 4:30 P.M. or so I left the house and drove to Lamberhurst. There was a lot of construction going on, but I was able to park my car and walk a bit. One thing I must learn about villages is that roads do not connect up. One cannot walk on one and expect there to be a connector to another. If you proceed one way, then you must return on the same route. I could tell that Lamberhurst is a lovely little village, but it sure was chewed up by all the roadwork. And as I was leaving, the pub that I intended to eat at, the Brown Trout, was on fire. There were three fire engines before it and people standing outside. I elected to press on.

I had my evening meal at the Swan, which was fine but, as John Petrie described it, it is a little ostentatious—at least the prices were. I settled for fried hake, which is a white fish, and chips of course. While eating I listened. First the barkeep dressed down a waitress for not cleaning up before leaving. That took a while because she had a reason for everything instead of just saying she was sorry. Then three gents, all dolled up in their suits, came in and stood at the bar, busily working on some deal. There were seats all around, but they wanted to stand and conduct business, right before me. I suppose they were tired of sitting all day.

I returned home around 7:30 P.M. or so and continued with my salt readings. I finished everything up and had a nice bath, but I unwisely also had two nice cups of tea that prevented me from assuming an easy sleep. I read some more in Stevenson, and I thought that would put me off, but it didn't. Thus, to bed at 10 P.M. and up at 7:30 A.M., a nice 9 1/2 hours of sleep! I have to get back into my old habit of being up with the light or I never will get anything done.

The Piltdown Man, Battle of Hastings, and Essex

I had a bit more activity on Wednesday, the 18th. After another filling breakfast I packed my gear together and said goodbye to Sunninglye, at least for a while. The first stop in my journey was Piltdown to see if there was any record of this site that is so important in the history of archaeology. As it turns out, there is hardly a record of the town itself! I was just about through it before realizing its insignificance. I pulled into a drive behind the local pub and talked to a man who was working on a car. He directed me to a public foot walk that would take me near the site of the finds, but I wouldn't actually be able to get to it he said, as the man who owns the vineyard doesn't like people tromping about (Figure 4). I noted that the pub is called the "Piltdown Freehouse" and

Figure 4. The Piltdown Man's remains were found at the end of this pasture near the line of trees.

Figure 5. A pub called the Piltdown Man Freehouse is about the only indication that an important site is located nearby.

its sign is an artist's rendition of the Piltdown Man (Figure 5), but otherwise the only thing that would give an indication of this once important find, the discovery that quite literally rocked the world and put Piltdown on the map, is a battered sign that reads "Piltdown Accommodations."

As I was preparing to leave the village, the same mechanic mentioned that if I was interested there is a building in nearby Uckfield that I might want to visit. It is called Dawson Hart Solicitors and was started by two men, one of whom was Charles Dawson, the discoverer of the Piltdown finds (Figure 6). I went there and the receptionist directed me to a box that was enclosed by a curtain. Within it was a plaster cast of the famous head (Figure 7). I felt as if I was seeing a relic. A label that bears elaborate calligraphy sits next to the box. It tells the story of how the British Museum awarded the fabricated skull to this firm in 1969. And I bet they were glad to be rid of this embarrassing chapter in their history. Is Conan Doyle still laughing? I wonder. [7]

---

[7] Conan Doyle is my choice as the culprit for the Piltdown hoax (Winslow and Meyer 1983), though many others have been accused over the years.

Figure 6. The Dawson Hart Solicitors building in Uckfield. Charles Dawson was the finder of Piltdown Man.

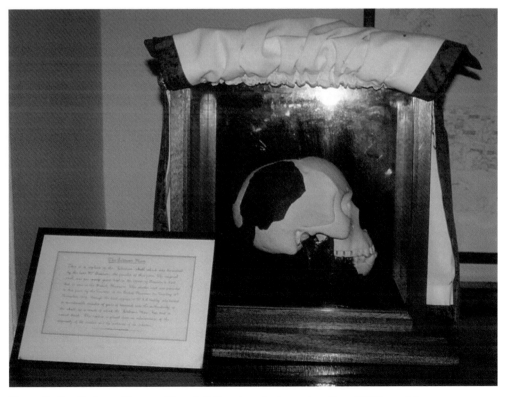

Figure 7. On display at Dawson Hart Solicitors is a plaster cast replica of Piltdown Man.

From Uckfield I went south and east to the village of Battle, as I wanted to walk the fields of the Battle of Hastings. The National Trust puts on a pretty good show, as usual. I paid my 5 bob, got a recorder, and headed out on the grounds. There were lots of school children scurrying about but, thankfully, they always kept to the short route and had far more pleasure exploring the ruins of Battle Abbey than they did learning about an ancient tussle. William the Conqueror constructed this Benedictine abbey on the field of battle, in part to atone for his killing of Harold and so many Saxons. The now-destroyed altar in the church, courtesy of Henry VIII, was set on the very spot where Harold met his maker, so it's told (Figure 8).

The battlefield itself is very small (Figure 9). The landscape obviously worked in favor of the Saxons, so one wonders what the Normans could have been thinking of? The high hill on the north was occupied by Saxon troops and far below them in a basin–shaped valley were the Normans, Bretons, and Flemish warriors. By position alone the odds were certainly against William and his men, but the invaders did have some advantages over the Saxons. First, the Normans themselves were professional soldiers, raised from birth to fight. Second, they had greater motivation (at least I think so), as the Crown

Figure 8. The square stone that sits before the ruins of Battle Abbey is supposedly the spot where the Saxon King Harold was killed at the Battle of Hastings.

Figure 9. A nice model of the Battle of Hastings occurs at the beginning of the tour. The Saxons occupied the hill on the left at the time of the battle. It now supports Battle Abbey's ruins.

Figure 10. When only infantry was involved, the Saxons had the advantage over the Normans simply because of their position on the hill.

was promised to William and he seems to have been cheated out of it. Third, they had mounted knights. And fourth, they had archers. The Saxons did have horses, but they didn't waste them in warfare, as they were far too valuable in farming. The most commonly used offensive weapon for the Saxons was the battleaxe, and the shield was their armor. A solid line of shields on the crest of the hill certainly couldn't have instilled much confidence in William's troops (Figure 10).

Although the presence of archers would seem to be a distinct advantage, without constant reinforcement they are not all that effective in battle. For archers to have an impact, it is imperative that both sides have them. Otherwise once a quiver is empty, that's it. I hadn't really thought about it before, but an archer probably spent most of his time on a battlefield picking up the arrows that the opposing side had already shot. And if the Saxons didn't shoot any, then the archers must have been at a loss as to what to do. The difference in this battle is that reinforcements eventually did come and their quivers were repacked, which is the real reason for the success of the Normans.

Harold's Saxon warriors had just returned from a heavy march and were exhausted. They had been in Yorkshire defeating another group that was allied with William, but there was no time to rest. Although they did have the field advantage, it was the Normans who had promise of reinforcements if only they could hold on. If Harold was to win, he had to do so early in the day. The Saxons did have a few charges against William's forces, but each charge failed. The Normans simply feigned retreat and then stopped. Then the knights took over by encircling the flanks of the Saxon warriors.

After several hours of stalemate play, it became clear that victory depended on which king fell first. Both were heavily engaged in the actual fighting. In those days, when there were only 7,000 or so on a side, which seems a ludicrously small number for such a momentous event, the king was not only a symbol, but an important war leader as well. Of the two, William fell first and this almost gave way to a major panic. Somewhat dazed, he got back on his horse, took off his helmet, and cheered, thus giving his troops new incentive. Harold's fall came in the late afternoon when the newly armed archers were moved to the front lines. They were instructed to shoot above the line of shields on the hillcrest so that their arrows would fall upon the unarmed soldiers in the background. Sadly enough for the Saxons, one of these individuals was Harold. The arrow that entered Harold's eye changed the course of history. As he fell, so too did Saxon England. The Saxons did continue to fight that day and for weeks after, but without a king their efforts were fruitless.

Figure 11. It is amazing just how small the battlefield was at the Battle of Hastings, especially considering the impact of this conflict in the history of England.

Long after the battle was over William stayed on the field, well into the evening it seems. His soldiers eventually found Harold's mutilated body, but William would not permit its return, lest the Saxons use it as a relic. The idea of using body parts as holy relics was already established by the Catholic Church and William obviously knew the symbolic power that human bones possessed. Though insensitive, he really was wise not to let them have their leader's corpse.

It's amazing to conceive that England has not been invaded successfully since the Battle of Hastings, only three score years shy of a millennium (Figure 11). What a different world we live in now where never would a king, a president, or a dictator expose himself on a field of battle. Perhaps we would have far less war if they did.

By about 3 P.M. I was back on the road and headed for Essex. It was a longer trip than I expected, and once I did get on to the M25 around London the roads were very congested. The most interesting part was going under the Thames River via a tunnel. I was not prepared for that and began to wonder if the

Figure 12. Broman's Farm B&B in East Mersea, Essex.

people on the other side would be speaking French. I got to Colchester around 5 P.M. in time for their rush hour and eventually found my way to Mersea Island. I checked in to Broman's Farm (Figure 12) and met the proprietors, Martin and Ruth Dence. After unpacking and having some tea before a fire that Martin made in the study, I took a walk up to the Dog and Pheasant Pub and had a lamb liver dinner. It was much more than I anticipated, however, and I was uncomfortable all through the night. My room is quite nice though and I have it set up whereby I can get some work done. Before going to bed I reread Paul R. Sealey's article on some recent Briquetage finds.[8]

Studying Briquetage at the Colchester Museum

I had a nice solid breakfast at 8 A.M. on the morning of the 19th, enough to tide me over until dinner (Figure 13). One thing about these heavy morning meals is that I do not feel at all hungry come noon. I left the farm around 9:15 A.M. and drove the seven miles to Colchester without mishap. I even made it with-

---

[8] Sealey 1995.

Figure 13. A massive fireplace brings comfort to the dining room at Broman's Farm where I had my daily breakfast.

out problem to High Street. My troubles began when I missed my turn on to Museum Street, as I did not expect it to be such a small thoroughfare. Little did I realize when I turned off to the left that it would be another half hour before I even made it back to High Street. Thus, I ended up getting to the parking lot behind the Museum Resource Centre around 10:15 A.M., just fifteen minutes early.

I checked in to the Centre and Dr. Sealey came down to meet me (Figure 14). He is a very obliging sort and just delighted to help me with my work. To have someone come all the way from Alabama, U.S.A., to see their collections is not something that occurs very often, if ever. He had set aside two days to assist me, which was very good of him. The archaeology storage area is located at a considerable distance from the Centre, at least half a mile from the Castle across a park and in a somewhat dilapidated warehouse.[9] Dr. Sealey set me up on the top floor where I not only had ample workspace, but good lighting from the skylight. He then showed me the shelves upon shelves of briquetage boxes

---

[9] Dr. Sealey was very apologetic for the conditions and explained that they were moving to a new facility soon. I assured him, however, that I had been in far worse places.

Figure 14. Dr. Paul R. Sealey, Curator of Archaeology at the Colchester Museum, was a great aid to my research in 2005.

from various sites and left me to my own devices to start exploring (Figures 15 and 16). I concentrated on the Langenhoe and Goldhanger districts, as I had read the archaeological reports on those sites. I looked at pedestals, firebars, wedges, troughs, and massive sections of hearths, all extremely dusty. It was a job just keeping my camera clean in the process. I kept a bucket of water and some towels near to hand, so that I could wash up between bouts of analysis.

I was especially intrigued by the size difference in artifacts between sites in the Goldhanger and Langenhoe districts. The former are so large that they look as if they have been on hormones. It started to rain in the late afternoon, which was rather depressing as I had left my raincoat in the car. Fortunately, it was drizzling just a little as we walked back to the Resource Centre. I decided to stay in the city for dinner in order to avoid the rush hour. Plus, I needed to buy some Ordnance Survey maps of the region to aid me in my upcoming seawall walks. I bought Nos. 176 (Blackwater Estuary) and 184 (Colchester), as those would give me ample coverage. As I strolled about the city of Colchester, I watched all the shops close, almost simultaneously it seemed. It would not have surprised me had they began to roll up the sidewalks in this mass exodus

Figure 15. The Essex Red Hills material was stored on the top floor of the Colchester Museum's warehouse in 2005.

Figure 16. The author busily measures firebars in the Colchester Museum's holdings.

from the city. I don't know why this astonished me, as Nancy and I observed these city shutdowns years ago in Lancaster and York, and I even commented on it at the time in my journal.[10]

I ended up eating at a Mediterranean restaurant, but I did not choose my dish wisely. I should remember that I really do not like strips cut from hanging meat. I'm not really sure as to what this heavily seasoned meat is (they said it's lamb), but I know it's not to my taste. However, the waitress was. She was an adorable brunette with a very shapely figure. Noting her accent I asked what country she hailed from? Ah, Russia, which did not surprise me. Why is it that women are so beautiful in Russia? This is especially so in the St. Petersburg district, which turned out to be her home. We chatted for a while and she seemed delighted that someone took an interest in her. She is in Colchester with her boyfriend and they are both studying at the University. It did not sound as if she would be returning to her home any time soon, which seems to be the pattern for those who emigrate from Russia.

I had a quick ride back to Mersea Island, as the traffic had largely disappeared by 7 P.M. After dropping off my things, I settled down to read Kay De Brisay's report on "The Excavation of a Red Hill at Peldon,"[11] but I got distracted from that when a new boarder arrived. He sat before the fire, too, drinking his cup of tea. His name is Nigel Hughes and he is an architect from Dorset. We exchanged cards and, as we continued to talk, we learned that we have archaeological interests in common, as well as shared friends. He wrote a book called *Maya Monuments* in 2000, which is chock full of his watercolors. He is a friend of Ian Graham and knows Dan Jones, too, both at the Peabody Museum and old friends of mine. Ian even attended the opening celebration of Hughes' book. We talked for a while and I then retired for the evening to finish reading the De Brisay article and to bathe. It was a full day, a good one to be inside because of the rain.

Friday was another dismal day, but I was to be inside, so no matter. I visited with Mr. Hughes at breakfast some more and discovered other things about him. In addition to being an architect, an artist, a Mayan enthusiast, and an ornithologist, he is also a maker of Memorials. He has carved several tombstones as part of his resume, which set us off on a discussion of cemeteries. He gave me the names of several of his friends in Cambridge to contact, but I doubt that I will be able to do so, as I do not have much time.

---

[10]   That would have been September 7, 1982.
[11]   DeBrisay 1974.

At 9:30 A.M. I met up with Dr. Sealey once more. He photocopied De Brisay's Peldon Red Hill article for me and arranged for me to buy Fawn et al.'s book on *The Red Hills of Essex: Salt-Making in Antiquity*.[12] A local bookstore fortunately still has a copy available as it has been out of print for 15 years. We then returned to the storage unit and I worked continuously until 5 P.M. on the collections. All totaled, I examined 26 boxes. He said that no one in his memory had worked so diligently without break and it was clear to him that I was enjoying it, which I truly was. I think I have seen just about all of the various renditions of the equipment making up Essex briquetage, but I'm now not so certain about how the objects functioned. It was far easier to understand things from the literature alone. Now that I've seen the artifacts, I'm not so sure that all that has been said about them is true. I wish that somewhere firebars could be found in place, for example, because I now know that it is not a simple matter of them having been pushed into the sidewalls of hearths to support troughs. From what I have seen of the few extant hearth wall sockets, the angle of orientation does not match well with the way the firebars are supposed to have been arranged…. Clearly, there are still many puzzles involving the Red Hills, and a few test pits here and there are not going to resolve the issue. What are needed are more full-scale excavations on the order of those conducted by the Red Hills Explorations Committee or by De Brisay and the members of the Colchester Archaeological Group. Unfortunately, there are no government funds for such, so it would have to be a privately funded research project.

I walked down to the Castle Bookstore to buy my book, but despite the fact that I had got there just before closing time (5:30 P.M.), it was already closed. That was frustrating, because I really need to have that volume for the time that I am in England. I walked around Colchester a bit more before departing. I have mixed feelings about the city. It certainly has some picturesque spots, particularly its narrow winding alleys on the south side of the hill, but there are also some rather seedy areas. The lower portion of Queen Street, for example, seems to be a hangout for riffraff. High Street is the principal thoroughfare, but beyond the Castle and the George Hotel, I did not see anything along it that captured my attention. Truthfully, though, I have only seen Colchester in the rain and during after hours, immediately after the disappearance of its population. I have not done it the justice it deserves.

This time I did not stick around to eat in town. Instead, I drove south to Mersea Island. I headed to West Mersea, expecting to see a pleasant little fish-

---

[12] DeBrisay 1978a and Fawn et al. 1990.

ing village or tourist town. In that I was disappointed as it seems to be a bedroom community for Colchester. There is nothing quaint about it at all. East Mersea, on the other hand, has "country" in its favor. In looking for a place to eat, I drove off the island once more and stopped at the Peldon Rose for a pub meal. This was a little too swank for my plebian tastes, as I am on a tight budget. Almost every table was reserved anyways, so I decided to try elsewhere. It is a pretty place though and I'm sure the food is good. Had it been warmer, it would have been pleasant to eat outside. I ended up having my meal at the Hasken's Restaurant next to the village shop and post office in East Mersea. There I had a nice minced beef and onion pie with a vegetable medley of peas, potatoes, carrots and broccoli. A lemon pudding saturated in custard finished off the feast. I am glad I'm only eating two meals a day or I would be a complete roly-poly by the end of the trip. I settled in the den when I got back to Broman's Farm and "read at" *Season to Taste* by Colin Dence,[13] father of Martin. He is a nice easy writer and imparts a lot of wisdom with regard to the history and use of seasonings. Unfortunately, though, he did not write much on the subject of salt.

The Red Hills of the Goldhanger District

First thing Saturday morning I stopped at the East Mersea village store to get some plastic bags, in the event that I actually found something in my survey. The saleswoman didn't have any and directed me to the Coop in West Mersea, which is a nice little grocery store. I'm sure they think it is enormous though. It is so much more civilized than ours in the States, what with the cashiers sitting at their task. The checkout counters are arranged in such a way for the ease of their workers, which seems so logical. I also bought some shampoo and a small box of laundry soap there. Then I drove back into Colchester to buy the *Red Hills of Essex* book, but first I had to come to terms with the parking situation. It all makes good sense once you've figured it out, but unless you're coming back to the same place again, you can't use the acquired knowledge.

The Castle Bookstore boasts 45,000 volumes, and I can well believe it. They certainly have the best selection of archaeology books that I have ever seen at a bookstore, new or used. In addition to the Essex book on salt-making, I purchased four other books: *Archaeology in British Towns: from the Emperor Clau-*

---

[13] Dence 1985.

Figure 17. The main excavation area at Goldhanger VIII (RH176), as seen from the north-northeast.

dius to the Black Death, by Patrick Ottaway; *Archaeology in the Field,* by O. G. S. Crawford; *Flights into Yesterday,* by Leo Deuel; and *The Archaeology of Medieval England,* by Helen Clarke. The total cost was 50 pounds (approximately $100), which wasn't bad for these five out-of-print books, but as they didn't accept American Express (who does?), I had to walk up the hill to find an ATM machine. The good thing about doing so was that I learned I could get money out of the ATM machine in England whenever I need it; prior to today this was assumed, but untested.

I got to the village of Goldhanger at around noon and headed off on a five-hour sojourn along the seawall. I had originally intended to go east, but once I saw location VIII[14] off to my right, I was drawn in that direction. Although it sits below the seawall, it is the only raised area around and that was no doubt the reason why it was selected as the site of a sailing club facility (Figure 17). It supports a flimsy two-story wooden building in the center of a grassy plot. The boats, all rather small, are upended and arranged along the edge of the field. A member named Mike Newport permitted me to come on the grounds and look

---

[14] See Reader 1910a for locations.

around, which was most kind of him. In the approximate center of the grounds is a large concrete platform, which housed an antiaircraft gun during WWII, and behind it is a raised earthen wall, presumably a remnant of the old saltern. One can still see numerous depressions throughout the grounds, the result of the Red Hills Exploration Committee's investigations in 1908. This was the location of some of the most intricate excavation work conducted by this team. They found numerous sets of long trenches on top of this small hill, which they interpreted as flues. Their overall conclusion was that the intrusive trenches related to salt production during the Roman period, but that the briquetage itself related to earlier Iron Age enterprises. As of 2005, it is still not clear who actually constructed these trenches.

I actually did not gain access to the grounds of Goldhanger VIII until the end of the day, as my strategy is to first make the walk, observing as I go, and then come back by the same route and make photos and written records. This way I have already made a selection of best views and what things merit recording. The key of course is to return along the same path, which I thought would be tedious. It is not, though, because obviously one sees a very different scene on the reverse route (Figure 18).

Midway on my walk I got saturated by a downpour. The wind was wild throughout the day and every once and a while a cloud would let loose. This

Figure 18. The inlet that divides Goldhanger VI (RH175) and VIII (RH176) was high and dry during the first half of my journey.

Figure 19. The causeway to Osea Island is open only at low tide.

particular blast lasted twenty minutes or so and my pants were absolutely soaked. I had thought to bring my raincoat, but I was totally unprepared as regards waterproof leggings; they sat snugly in my suitcase in the closet. Nevertheless, once the rain stopped, the sun and wind dried me out and I reentered a comfort zone. I made it as far west as the caravan parks just outside of Maldon. It was here that the first of the Goldhanger (I) Red Hills occur, just to the east of Osea Road. Could this be the hill that De Brisay explored in her 1972 and 1973 publications? Probably so, but as I do not yet have those works, I cannot say for sure.[15] I did see a rise in the approximate location of where it is supposed to be by virtue of the Reader 1910a article, but I have no way of knowing for sure.

The causeway that leads out to Osea Island is intriguing. It is only functional during low tide and it winds in serpentine fashion as it makes its way out to the island (Figure 19). I suppose that the curves are purposeful, because if they had made the road straight certain idiots would try to pass when it's inundated. Only the hardy, the foolhardy that is, would make such an attempt on the current road. The denizens of the island must have to plan their shopping ventures to the mainland carefully.

---

[15] I later discovered that this is indeed the site that De Brisay excavated, Osea Road (RH 184).

Figure 20. The Fleet occurs in front of Goldhanger IX (RH171). Agricultural fields or pasture in the dry areas protected by the seawall obscure evidence of Essex Red Hill sites.

Figure 21. The Chequers Inn at Goldhanger offered a nice respite at the end of the day.

With the exceptions of Locations I and VIII, I was unable to relocate any of the other Red Hills of Goldhanger on my survey today (Figure 20). I know that I was either standing on them or looking at them, as most of them are plotted on the Ordnance map, but one would have to know that they are there. Agriculture has certainly taken its toll in reducing the sites to mere patches of reddish soil on the landscape, and it is only red when it's wet. Otherwise it just blends in with everything else. Rain notwithstanding I did enjoy the walk.

It was about 5:30 P.M. when I got back to my car, which was parked near the Chequers Inn (Figure 21). I dropped off my gear, grabbed my fieldbook and headed into the pub for some quiet time. With a pint of Titanic beer and a nice small round table at my convenience, I proceeded to take notes. The final minutes of a soccer match were underway, so it was not as quiet as I have made it out to be, but it was comfortable nonetheless. People started to flow in as it approached the 6:30 P.M. dinner hour. I'm sure they must have wondered who the crazy guy was who had maps sprawled out in front of him and was writing furiously. I must have been a curiosity. I eventually ordered a meal, too, but decided to go cheap, with a "Chequers Big Burger." It was a match for Ruby Tuesday's or Appleby's in terms of size and I elected to eat only half of it. Even then I was full, and remember, I have not been eating lunches. Between ample breakfasts and dinners like these, however, my girth is not declining whatsoever. Several more walks like today will surely start to have an impact.

I'm glad that I persevered with the Goldhanger District as it finally paid off. Sunday morning I was trying to decide whether to walk the northern part of Mersea Island or return to Goldhanger. The advantage of the former was proximity, as it was Sunday and I was very low on gas, but from what I could tell from the *Red Hills of Essex* book, most of the Mersea Red Hills are far inland away from the sea wall. Thus, I would have a nice walk, but probably never see a site. Goldhanger had more possibilities, as the sites are clearly marked in the vicinity of the sea wall, and yet I had already come to the conclusion that most of them have been leveled by cultivation. The photographs I have taken show nice even fields (Figure 22), so I will be hard pressed to convince my students that they are looking at salt production sites. And yet, it would be nice to at least finish the Goldhanger district, if only to say I had walked the entire coast from Tollesbury to Maldon—twice! On this basis, I decided to return to Goldhanger.

I started my walk at 10 A.M. from the churchyard. Most people were entering the handsome flint stone building, but I passed them by, preferring instead God's natural home. I made my way across the field, artfully dodging piles of

Figure 22. Goldhanger VI (RH175) occurs in the center of the picture, with the village of Goldhanger in the background. Although a slight rise is visible in the field, one would not really know it was a Red Hill site without having a map.

Figure 23. A classic example of "saltings" at low tide can be observed south of Goldhanger III (RH180) and IV (RH179), as seen from the south-southwest.

excrement left by leashed canines and eventually ended up back at the inlet where I left off on Saturday. Rain threatened all day, but it never did come, which was just fine with me. This time I brought my waterproof pants in my knapsack, and there they sat. The walk east was long and unprofitable, but I did enjoy the many sights, if not sites (Figure 23). The tide was coming in and there was a very strong wind coming out of the west, so my walk was assisted somewhat. I didn't dare spread my arms and jump or I would have flown off the sea wall. There were a lot of sailboats out on the River Blackwater taking advantage of a Sunday breeze. I say "river," but when the tide is in the whole region resembles a bay. Only when the tide turns is it possible to see banks. Surprisingly, Goldhanger Creek actually does become a creek at that time too.

The tide was about at its height when I approached Goldhanger XIII on the extreme eastern end of the district just to the south of Tollesbury (Figure 24). Archaeologically speaking, I was very depressed as a few specks on a small patch of earth at Goldhanger XI constituted my only evidence for briquetage. As I left that site at about 1 P.M. or thereabouts and proceeded west, I remember thinking how quickly the tide had turned. Less than an hour earlier the waters were lapping the upper edge of the sea wall, and now I could actually see

Figure 24. Tollesbury occurs in the distance with Goldhanger XIII (RH164) to the left in this picture, as seen from the south. The tide was at its height at the time, clearly showing the effect of sea walls in protecting the productive land.

Figure 25. When the tide was at its lowest, two probable weirs could be seen in the tidal flats at the head of Goldhanger Creek's northern branch. This is located just to the south of the Goldhanger V (RH177) location, as seen from the northwest.

Figure 26. This is the deposit that I first saw from the seawall when the tide was dropping. It is a fine example of how briquetage erodes out of Red Hill sites.

mud. If I chose to stay in one place for more than a few minutes, I was sure that I would see the shore drain like a tub. That's how rapidly it happened (Figure 25).

And then something caught my eye. On a gentle bank of alluvium there were reddish objects that looked like bricks (Figure 26). Tufts of marsh grass covered what seemed to be a slight rise behind the debris, enough to raise my curiosity and, also, my anticipation that I might have happened upon an unrecorded Red Hill. This would fall under the category of a "wet" one, because it was beyond the sea wall. As I walked off the seawall and approached it, my suspicions were justified. I noted a well-beaten path to the rise. Others had been there before, and often. I walked right out to the end where I could see that a cut bank occurred, a relatively steep one at least 1.5 m tall. As I peered over the edge I was delighted to see a narrow beach filled with briquetage. Getting a better view of the exposed bank, I could observe a mass of briquetage set within a red soil matrix, all sitting atop the blue-gray London Clay (Figures 27 and 28). I could even see a pit that was filled with patches of briquetage and charcoal. And nearby was another pit, circular in shape, which stood out from the beach. It was filled with yellowish-brown clay and had a dense patch of

Figure 27. The Tolleshunt d'Arcy Site (RH 168) is a well-preserved Red Hill, especially considering that it has been exposed to tidal effects for at least two millennia.

Figure 28. Briquetage can be seen eroding out of the solid red wall comprising the Tolleshunt d'Arcy Site (RH168).

charcoal and briquetage along its northern and western edges. The highlight was an exposed hearth of rectangular shape, more horseshoe perhaps, which opened to the southwest. And all around was briquetage. I picked through it carefully to find just the right objects to use in class instruction, and I only retrieved items from the beach itself. According to Dr. Sealey, who I queried on the subject, what lies beyond the sea wall falls under the category of "finders' keepers." I was only hoping to gather a representative sample, however, so just collected the base of a pedestal and a large rim sherd from a trough. I looked diligently, but was unable to find a firebar. That would have made my day, but the pedestal was good enough.

I ended up spending about an hour at the site, which I have come to learn is called Tolleshunt d'Arcy (RH 168), named after the parish. Apparently, I had left Goldhanger Parish somewhere between Goldhanger VII and IX. Now that I was aware of the site, no matter where I stood on the sea wall it was clearly visible. I looked out for other such edifices in the saltings on my way back, but without success. I did see the family of swans that I had sympathized with on the journey out, however. When I first saw them they were walking along the inside of a wire fence in search of a way to the water, which always was just beyond their reach. Now I discovered that they too had succeeded in their quest. They must have found some breech in the fence, as the parents and their cygnets were now playfully frolicking in the Fleet.

Off to my left was a long bank dense in marsh vegetation. Just as I was thinking how pristine it looked, nature devoid of humanity, a man popped his head out of the mass. He jerked his body and lifted a large wooden pole on to his shoulders, no doubt considered a blessed gift from the sea for this scavenger. Humans are everywhere, industrious to no end, doing strange and esoteric things. Some of them even walk seawalls in search of red soil (Figure 29).

I finally got back to my car at about 5 P.M., having spent seven hours hiking the district. It was tiring, but I was enervated by the success of finding a Red Hill, which at the time seemed to be an original discovery. I again took my notepad, map, and fieldbook and headed to the Chequers Inn. Unfortunately, although it was open for drink, they were not serving food, so I sensed disaster in the making. My breakfasts carry me through most of the day, but by 5–ish I am starting to get rather ravenous. It being Sunday, I was beginning to think that perhaps I would not find a meal anywhere. I knew that was the case to

Figure 29. There is still ample evidence for human use of the lands surrounding Red Hills, as seen by Joyce's Farm, viewed from the south-southeast.

the east, but perhaps Maldon would have a restaurant that was open. It was certainly worth the short trip, but I had to be very careful not to investigate too far. I was already down to less than 45 miles of gas in the tank (the car tells me what's left—what a great idea!)[16] and feared that I would not find a place open until Monday. It was 10 miles back to Broman's Farm from Goldhanger, so I really was cutting it close. Fortunately, I did find a fish and chips shop just as I entered Maldon. I ordered a medium-sized portion (I'm glad I didn't get large!) of fried cod. The woman poured vinegar and salt on it and wrapped it up in some paper. I ate it in the car and oh did it taste grand. I kept thinking about my Dad and how much he would have enjoyed the meal I was eating.

As I was leaving Maldon I noticed a Shell station with a line of cars, so I was able to take care of my other little problem. It turned out to be not so little. Thirty-nine pounds later, approximately $80, and I had just about filled up my tank. I almost had a coronary over the cost and was wondering if I was pumping the gas into a hole beneath the car. A tank of gas yields about 450 miles of gas in the car I was driving, which seems like a lot, but not when you reckon that's a little more than $1 for every five miles. It's worth planning one's trips very carefully, as there is little room for mistakes. Every wrong turn can be quite costly.

When I got back to the Farm I settled in the den and wrote my notes. I had not quite finished them by 9:30 P.M., but I decided it was time to retire anyways. As I turned off the light, I looked up at the stars. The Dences, my hosts, must have put some florescent dots on the ceiling to comfort weary travelers. I searched for the Big Dipper, but fell asleep before finding it.

Maldon Salt Works and Sutton Hoo

As of Monday, May 23, I have now been here but a week, and yet it seems like so much longer. That's the good thing about travel. Time expands. I am out of the field until Friday when I am scheduled to see a West Mersea site with Martin and Ruth Dence. My objectives today were to visit the Maldon Salt Works and to go to the Sutton Hoo site. The latter I accomplished; the former I did not. I shouldn't say that I didn't see the salt works, as I did observe the building, but even that wasn't easy. Everyone in town that I spoke to, five people to be exact, had a different opinion as to where it was. Most of them believed it was on the

---

[16]   It really is not a great idea. In the long run, all it did was make me very nervous.

Figure 30. The now-abandoned Malden Salt Works building.

quay, except for a bus driver, who had never even heard of it. I did a lot of trips to the quay on this bright and sunny morning, but only on my final attempt (because I really had had enough) did I meet my objective. Right across from the Rose and Crown Pub, not the Ship and Anchor, despite one old lady's insistence, is a narrow lane called Butt Street. It certainly was appropriately named, as I felt that I had been the butt of a nasty joke. I followed Butt Street until it came to a steep slope to the left. Gingerly entering that street, I happened upon a small dark building with a blackened chimney, the saltworks at last. Strangely enough, there was no one in the parking lot except for one red car. I parked mine next to it and approached the main office. I could see through the window, however, that all was vacant. They had moved! An operation that had been going for decades, perhaps centuries, had elected to pack up and shift to another location just prior to my visit. A fellow traveler of Butt Street explained to me how to get to the new salt works, but as he talked my eyes merely glazed over. I really didn't want to see the "new" works. I wanted to watch an age-old operation taking place in an equally antiquated building.[17] Considerably disgruntled by the turn of events, I satisfied myself with a picture of the building and made a hasty retreat from Maldon (Figure 30).

---

[17]   Soudah 1987.

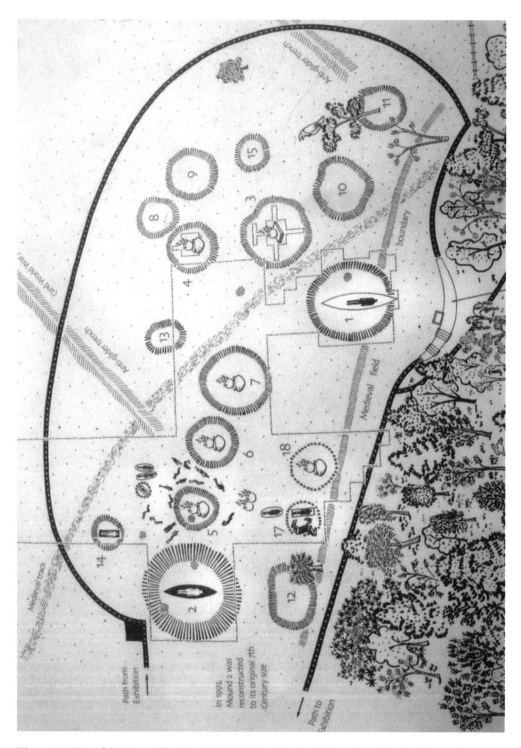

Figure 31. Map of the Sutton Hoo Site in Woodbridge showing the location of its burial mounds and other archaeological features.

To get to the famous Sutton Hoo site I traveled north to Ipswich and then on to Woodbridge. Sutton Hoo was excavated in 1939 when the lady of the estate, a Mrs. Pretty (who was not, by the way) commissioned an archaeologist named Basil Brown to excavate Mound 2 (Figures 31). Mrs. Pretty, it seems, was a somewhat superstitious lady so, when a friend of hers reported ghostly images arising from the barrows in a nearby field, she decided to investigate. To my way of thinking, the appearance of specters might have been more than enough reason to leave well enough alone, but Mrs. Pretty thought otherwise and the world is glad she did.

In the process of digging into Mound 2 (Figure 32), which is actually a rather piddling little mound as reconstructed, Mr. Brown came across iron rivets that were arranged linearly. It was evident that the rivets had once clamped together the boards of a ship's hull, so hopes were high they had come across a ship burial, which of course it was. At first Brown thought it might be a Vi-

Figure 32. Mound 2 at Sutton Hoo overlooks the individual graves of a man and his horse that were once situated beneath the now-removed Mound 17. Modern stone heaps mark the location of these two graves.

Figure 33. Mound 1 at Sutton Hoo, seen here in a restored state, once contained a ship burial.

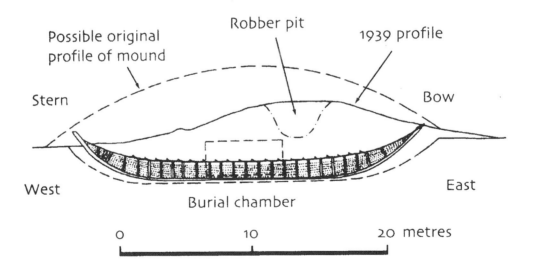

Figure 34. A profile of Mound 1 shows the location of the ship and burial chamber.

king burial, but the artifacts revealed an earlier event. It is now believed that the burial was of an Anglo-Saxon warrior king named Raewald, ruler of East Anglia. If that is true, the interment dates to A.D. 625.

Seventeen tumuli once existed in this elite Anglo-Saxon burial ground, spanning a period from A.D. 590 to 630. The largest mound, No. 1, had been looted in the distant past (Figures 33 and 34). It too was a ship burial, but in this case the body had been placed in a chamber beneath the vessel. Raewald's body (if there actually was a body—they're still not certain of that), on the other hand, had been placed within the boat. Moreover, all of his accoutrements were still there, an unbelievable oversight by the looters.

I spent quite a bit of time in the museum (Figure 35). The exhibits were so-so, but there was a lot of information in them that I wanted to read. I didn't like the video at all, because it is more designed to give one "a feel" for what it was like back then. It offered very little background on either the history of the site or its excavation. With a little effort, they could have done so much more.

Figure 35. The Sutton Hoo Museum has a rather dramatic entrance.

Figure 36. A life-size diorama of the Mound 1 ship burial is easily viewed by all visitors.

Figure 37. The Mound 1 ship burial is believed to have been an Anglo-Saxon king of East Anglia (c. A.D. 590-630).

However, I did like the full-scale reproduction of the burial chamber in the center of the exhibition hall (Figures 36 and 37), as well as their analytical treatment of the making of the various objects. The exhibit on sword construction was particularly edifying. Never again will I regard such objects as being "just swords."

After seeing a special exhibition on the mysterious hanging cauldrons, I took a walk around the grounds. The site actually reminds me of a small Hopewell mound center in the Ohio Valley. Mound 2 is the most impressive barrow of the lot. It sits in a saucer-shaped depression and has been totally reconstructed. Mound 1, which is best seen from the viewing platform, has a slight cleft in its middle. Presumably, they left the depression to give viewers the impression of a collapsed ship beneath the soil. A thick layer of grass covers the grounds and a dozen or so black-faced sheep were busily keeping things in order (Figure 38). While I was there a man was mowing around some graves in the vicinity of Mounds 5 and 17. The latter mound, now removed, once covered the graves of a man and his horse, both richly endowed with artifacts (see Figure 32).

Figure 38. Black-faced sheep roam the grounds at Sutton Hoo.

In the area around Mound 5 were the individual graves of people who had been buried at Sutton Hoo a couple of centuries after the Anglo-Saxon kings. In some ways, these are more intriguing than the mound burials. Because of the soil conditions at this site, all of their skeletal matter had disappeared. It was still possible to determine the arrangement and treatment of the bodies, however, because their flesh had fused with the sand. The excavators determined that all of these individuals met their maker in a violent fashion; not through warfare, but by torture and execution (Figure 39). All had received some form of bodily insults, including hanging, decapitation, and the like. The interpretation offered at the site is that Sutton Hoo continued to serve the community at around A.D. 800 as a spot for both the execution and burial of criminals. And that may be true, but something does not seem right. If Mrs. Pretty still retained a measure of superstition in the mid-twentieth century, I imagine that the ancient inhabitants of Woodbridge and Melton would have had respect or at least fear of the burial ground of their kings. It does not seem logical to me that a sacred site like Sutton Hoo would be used in such a profane manner. On the other hand, these people could have been sacrifices. That would be hard to distinguish from the execution of criminals, because they would have received the same kinds of treatment that are ob-

Figure 39. Exhibit signage on the grounds of Sutton Hoo reconstructs what the site is believed to have been like circa A.D 800. Most scholars interpret the disarticulated skeletons to be of criminals who were executed there.

served archaeologically. We have now come to think that most of the famous Bog burials were sacrifices of sorts, so maybe Sutton Hoo deserves further consideration with this line of thought.

When I got back to the reception building I bought a couple of postcards and ordered a pot of tea. That was refreshing and set me off on the road in good spirits. Leaving the old spirits behind was a good thing too. Instead of taking the busy A12 all the way into Colchester, I got off the dual carriageway in Ipswich and took the A137 south to Manningtree. That was nicer. Only later did I realize I was motoring through Constable Country, much nicer indeed!

I am starting to get a feel for the roads in and around Colchester, as I soon made my way to the Mersea Road and headed south. I was planning to settle in and then walk over to the Dog and Pheasant pub for dinner, but I had a sense that it might be closed for meals on Monday. I was correct. Fortunately, the Peldon Rose was open so I drove back off the island. I got there at 5:30 P.M., an hour before meal serving, so I ordered a pint and read snippets of English archaeology. I had a nice "lamb chump," which was served on a bed of ratatouille with a medley of vegetables. I must say that I do like the old part of Peldon Rose, but the conservatory is a bit too gentrified. I suppose they had to add this to keep up with their growing popularity, but it has spoiled the structure to my way of thinking. But then again, I'm not paying the bills.

When I got back to Broman's Farm I settled down in the den and lit a fire. Despite it being late in the month of May, it is still rather cool in both the day and night and the warmth of the fire felt very nice. I planned out my road trip to and from Cambridge for Tuesday and read another chapter in the *Red Hills of Essex* volume before retiring for the evening. Up at 6, breakfast at 8, dinner at 6:30, and lights out at 10:30—that has become my regular routine. If I take lunch it will kill me.

Cambridge and Thaxted, City and Town

Today, Tuesday the 24th, was devoted to visiting Cambridge, but it was far too much to do in a day, especially as it takes a couple of hours to get there. I could have done it in less, but that would have required taking the main highways. I prefer to take the back routes that go through villages, as I am not merely connecting points on a map in my travels. The "getting there" is as important, if not more important, than the destinations I have found. My trip to Cambridge consisted of taking the A134 from Colchester to Sudbury, and switching to the B1064 to the town of Cavendish. After skirting around Haverhill on the A1092, the A1307 then took me on into Cambridge.

I was able to find parking easy enough in the center of town, but the price after four hours was an astronomical jump, from 7 pounds to 13. Thus, I had to be back at the car by 3:30 P.M. to avoid losing my shirt. I suppose I could have driven out and right back in again, but as there was still much that I wanted to see in the countryside, four hours seemed to be more than enough time to see the University grounds and get a feel for the city. I couldn't have been further from the truth. By the time I next looked at my watch, it was past 2 p.m. and I realized I had hardly seen anything at all. But let's proceed in the order that my day unfolded.

I was delighted to observe, upon exiting the car park, that I was stationed at the Museum of Archaeology and Anthropology. I already had that on my agenda, so I decided to do it last just prior to departure. I sought out the City Information Center and found it nearby on the corner of Wheeler and Corn Exchange streets. There I bought what turned out to be a perfectly horrible map, and came to rely almost exclusively on directions posted at street corners. The Information Center wouldn't change a 50-pound note and neither would the nearby bank unless I was a member! I ended up at a foreign exchange institution down the street, wherein I was subjected to the silent tyranny of a cashier. The way he looked at my note, peering up through it at the light, you'd think I was trying to rob Lloyds of London. When he finally did make the exchange, I was seriously tempted to hold his two twenties and a ten up to the light in a similar manner. I refrained from doing so for fear that I might end up in the slammer for the rest of my Cambridge outing.

Well, that was half an hour wasted. Upon leaving the exchange I made my way to the King's Parade to see the College and Chapel. King's Chapel is the one thing to see in the city if you only have time for one thing. The foundations were laid by Henry VI, but it wasn't until Henry VII and VIII that it was finally completed. It is best known for its fan-vaulted ceiling, whatever that means, but one thing's for sure, it is beautiful, as are the stained glass windows. I would have enjoyed my time in this place of God far more if an elderly woman had not marked me from the first as someone she was going to irritate. Though small and wiry, she took up an inordinate amount of space. No matter where I stood or what I looked at, she always managed to edge her way in between. Had there not been witnesses, I most certainly would have stuffed her into an ancient vestment cabinet and lit a votive candle in her memory.

Upon emerging from the Chapel, I approached the Front Court of King's College (Figure 40). Examinations were in progress, so all walkways were off

Figure 40. A statue of Henry VI sits in the middle of the Front Court of King's College at Cambridge University.

limits to visitors. As I stood there in my blue rain jacket, with purple knapsack slung over my shoulder, and bulky Nikon camera around my neck, I must have looked a fool of a tourist. Students ambled by smiling and laughing, ignoring both the signs and the clearly irrelevant visitors. I wish now that when I was at Harvard as a student I had stopped to acknowledge some of the passersby. Many of these travelers must have been glad beyond belief just to be on hallowed ground and would, no doubt, have appreciated a little acknowledgement. I walked on, carefully avoiding stepping on the crew-cut grass of the Back Lawn. Off in the distance, on the other side of the River Cam, cows were lazily chewing their cud, all very picturesque, but strangely sterile without people in between. In all the vast patches of green, I never saw one person who ventured to sit upon it, touch it, or even stop to sniff the aroma of freshly cut grass. Students are allowed to tread upon the sacred lawns, but no one did, or at least not while I was there.

I paid 2 bob to enter Clare College, and I'm glad I did as that brought me right down to the river. Ah, to be a Master of a Cambridge College. He and his family occupied the northwest quadrant of this complex. The central portion consists of dorms (I assume), a Great Hall (for dining?), and a chapel. The courtyard is divided into quarters by walkways, all off limits of course ex-

Figure 41. The Scholars' Garden of Clare College. King's Chapel can be seen to the right.

Figure 42. Punters on the River Cam are viewed from the bridge at Clare College.

cept for the central path and the path to the chapel. I walked on through the back portico and noticed a plaque in honor of Paul Mellon. Apparently, this American philanthropist was a student at Clare in the 1930s and remained a generous benefactor for them over the years. The Master's residence is clearly marked on the door that comes off this portico. Behind his living quarters is a beautiful spacious garden; no visitors allowed, naturally. But those in my lot could go into the Scholars' Garden (Figure 41), which is situated immediately opposite on the south side of the walk. The wall that divides this garden from King's Lawn is reputedly one of the oldest in Cambridge.

From the bridge at Clare College, which is the oldest span across the Cam, I watched punters make their way up and down the river (Figure 42). None of them fared too well, however, as the wind was frightful. The steersman of each vessel had a job just to keep out of the drink. The Fellows' Garden, which is just opposite the Master's Garden (all highly structured socially), is large and beautiful (Figure 43). I would have loved to spend more time in it, but it was here that I examined my watch and was startled to see the hour. I still had two museums to visit!

Figure 43. The Fellows' Garden of Clare College is situated on the opposite side of the River Cam from the Master's Garden and is open to the public.

Figure 44. Entrance to the Museum of Archaeology and Anthropology at Cambridge University.

I made my way down Trumpington Street, past Corpus Christi College (my what a beautiful courtyard) and finally emerged at the Museum of Archaeology and Anthropology (Figure 44). It didn't open until 2 P.M., so my timing actually turned out to be perfect. There are three floors to this museum. The first is totally devoted to archaeology, and it covers the world. It is very object oriented, as might be expected, and there is generally a single bay devoted to each area or country. The amount that they have on display is really quite impressive, though it is of little use to anyone who is not a student or other form of researcher. Most people just rushed through the exhibits expressing appropriate oohs and ahs, as did I. On the second floor are the ethnology collections, again organized according to cultural areas, but there does not seem to be any real rhyme or reason to the arrangement. These exhibits are old overall and the display techniques are more in keeping with a mid-twentieth century philosophy. Nevertheless, it was nice to see some precious artifacts, including a giant Haida Indian totem pole (Figure 45) collected by C. F. Newcombe and a somewhat smaller one in the likeness of a grizzly bear from a Kwakiutl village, also a Newcombe acquisition. He sure did distribute his collections far and wide. The third floor of the museum, which is actually a mezzanine, is their changing exhibit gallery. It is here where they are being more innovative. There are

Figure 45. Ethnographic exhibits in the Museum of Archaeology and Anthropology include a Haida totem pole.

fewer artifacts, more words, and more visuals in these exhibits. From the vista of the mezzanine I was delighted to see a wooden sign labeled "Maudslay Hall," which hangs from the second floor ceiling. Presumably this is Alfred Maudslay, the great Mayan archaeologist and maker of stela casts. I wonder where they all are now?

In the time that I had remaining I made a quick tour of the Sedgewick Museum, which occupies the other corner of the building. To get to it one climbs a stairway into a tower. Immediately one enters a world of fossils. Cabinets upon cabinets present the life of the past from every region and time period imaginable. All the labels are carefully scribed on miniature pieces of paper that record genus, species, collector, and provenance. They seem to be of nineteenth-century vintage primarily. The objects are arranged in angled glass-topped displays, below which are multiple wooden shelves of systematic collections, all locked of course. This is definitely a student/researcher based exhibit, the displays seemingly just about as old as some of the fossils. Things get a bit newer and more publicly oriented to the right of the entrance after turning the corner, but even here it is best for the viewer to focus on just one or two things. There is no attempt to introduce the general visitor to geology, of either the Cambridgeshire region or the world. One better come into this

Figure 46. A typical gingerbread-like house in the village of Thaxted, Essex County.

place with some background knowledge, because one certainly does not leave with any. To be just, this is not a museum for a quick visit like mine. If I was willing or able to stay for a prolonged period, I know I would gain much from the experience. Thankfully, there still are museums like the Sedgewick and the Museum of Archaeology and Anthropology for people who do want to come back repeatedly to learn. For all others, there needs to be something else, but perhaps not here.

I made it back to my car with time to spare and was very fortunate to emerge from Cambridge with no wrong turns. I made my way south along the A1307 once more to Linton and then turned on to the B1052 to Saffron Walden. At this last town I got on to the B184 and headed toward Great Dunnow. Along the way I stopped at the little village of Thaxted for a cream tea (Figure 46). I just felt like one, that's all, and this was my first break in diet on the trip. My small repast occurred at a pub called Parishes. The lady who served me my tea and scone directed me to places to eat in West Mersea. Apparently, I had wronged that community, as there is more to it than I imagined. "Go to the Coast Inn for mussels," she said. "They're out of this world." Across the road from the Parishes was the Guildhall (Figure 47), a marvelous timber-frame structure. I photographed it as well as the adjoining "Dick Turpin's Cottage"

Figure 47. The Guildhall in Thaxted is an ancient building.

Figure 48. Behind the Guildhall is the so-called "Dick Turpin's Cottage."

(Figure 48) and then walked through the community. I even saw and photographed the windmill, high on the hill behind the churchyard. I really do need to spend more time in villages like this, and less time in a car.

When I got to Mersea Island, I decided to follow up on the above tip. I went right to the end of the road in West Mersea to find the Coast Inn, but I lost confidence and kept giving up too soon. Therefore, I had to do a lot of backtracking. I finally did find the restaurant, but they were out of mussels, the subject of my quest. They not only lacked mussels on the daily menu, but they pretty much lacked seafood altogether. I found this to be rather strange for a "Coast Inn," but it certainly was in keeping with my experiences in West Mersea. I decided to go elsewhere in the village for my mussels, settling in at a pub just up the road. The barkeeper there cheerfully informed me that they plan to start serving food in a week or two. My rumbling stomach obviously could not wait for that, so I bid my "final adieu" to West Mersea and headed for the rural East, to my old standby the Dog and Pheasant Pub. I knew without question that they had mussels on the menu there, and they did—on the menu. With all due apologies, I was told there were none in the larder, so that was it for mussels and me. I had a bowl of broccoli and Stilton soup with some French bread and considered myself most fortunate.

London

I had an appointment to meet up with my cousin, Tom Clare, at 4 P.M. on Wednesday at the Burlington House, so this was my "London Day." And if I thought four hours was too little for Cambridge, with London I would have needed years. In my last visit to London in 1990 I was not too impressed, but what a difference fifteen years have made. I have now fallen in love with that city, but in keeping with this narrative, first I had to get there.

Wisely electing not to drive, I parked my car at North Station in Colchester and took the 10 A.M. fast train west, the one that connects London and Norwich. Had I gone on the previous train I would have had to pay much more, as they stick it to commuters. The ride took about an hour through some very unmemorable countryside. I chose not to bring a book so that I could enjoy the scenes, but how was I to know? I also did not bring a camera, which was a very wise decision indeed. Otherwise I would not have advanced much beyond Tower Bridge. My mission today was to walk; to walk solidly up and down the streets of London, avoiding all forms of public transport, except for the return to Colchester. And that's what I did.

At Liverpool Street Station, where I started out, I bought a good map of the city, one that I could put in my back pocket with ease, and then I set off down Bishopsgate to The Monument. This structure was erected soon after the 1666 fire that destroyed much of London. What with the plague but a year earlier, the people must have started to question whether they actually were God's chosen. Ironically, disasters always seem to strengthen churches, as folk praise the lord at their good fortune for not being among the stricken. Priests and politicians seem to get good mileage out of holocausts of some sort.

I took a left on to Eastcheap and then proceeded down Great Tower St. until I came to All Hallows Church. It perhaps should have been called "All Gallows" because public executions were held just beyond it on Tower Hill. I was curious to learn that John Quincy Adams was married within this church. I wonder how that came about? I did not go in the Tower of London this time as I had already toured it twice in my life, but I was amazed at the transformation of the grounds to the west of it. Now that it has become a World Heritage site, they have made it into a grand park. It's a little like entering Disneyland, but I don't mean that in a derogatory fashion. They have learned to handle groups better, which is very important in London. The largest comparable city I have been in[18] is New York, but London has it beat for visitors. The city literally "rocks" from one end to the other with tourists, not least of which are school groups. All natures of language and colors of people are walking the streets of London at any one time in one vast patchwork quilt of humanity.

I walked out on to the Tower Bridge to get a better view of the city and of the Thames. There is now an exhibition on the bridge itself, which I would have loved to see, but I had chosen to walk on this tour, confining my views to mere "pop ins." I circled the Tower of London on my return to the city center and retraced my steps to The Monument. From there I continued along Cannon Street in the direction of St. Paul's Cathedral. What struck me most in this busy section of London is the number of people dressed in dark pinstripe suits. This includes both men and women, and the former often wear very colorful ties of pink and purple. Admittedly, it was lunch hour, so there were masses of professionals out on the street, but this attire was pretty consistent throughout the day, and a significant change from what I remember in 1990. Then there seemed to be a far rougher attire and London overall seemed noisier and dirtier. It is an active city to be sure, and active cities show the full-scale of life, but it is a much cleaner and neater place as of 2005.[19]

I wonder about the cost of the clothes people wear. If they were anywhere in the realm of what I was seeing in the shops' windows, then there are an awful lot of rich people walking the streets of London. I saw shoes that cost two to three hundred pounds and watches that were in the thousands of pounds. I do realize that we have such stores on New York's Fifth Avenue, but in London they seem to be everywhere.

I walked around St. Paul's Cathedral and ventured into the basement to visit their Gents' room. It seemed sacrilegious to do so, but I was desperate. To make reparations, I purchased a couple of postcards before venturing back to the streets. From St. Paul's I continued my westerly jaunt down Fleet Street. I popped in to the Cheshire Cheese Pub, which has been occupied continuously since 1667. Had it not been for the fire (it was rebuilt a year after this event), it would have had a much greater pedigree. That's a place that I definitely want to have a meal in the next time I return to London. When I got to Waterloo Bridge

---

[18]   Western cities, that is. Beijing is certainly of comparable size to London, but it is very different in other ways.

[19]   I later learned that the changes in London have much to do with fees now charged on personal vehicles that enter the city. As a result of such, people are taking public transportation more frequently and this has reduced the hubbub significantly.

I took it, this time actually crossing the river. I turned right toward Jubilee Gardens and came across the most impressive Ferris wheel that I have ever seen, the "London Eye." British Airways made it, which is certainly appropriate as the structure reaches to the clouds. As with the original Ferris wheel, which graced the 1893 Columbian Exposition in Chicago, each "car" is enormous. I could not really tell from my vantage point, but I imagine the individual cars carry between twenty and twenty-five people. Slowly the wheel turns, taking about a half hour to make a complete revolution. On a clear day like today one could probably see Paris! I seriously contemplated paying the 12.50 pounds ($25) for the experience, but elected to keep to my agenda, adding the London Eye to my list of things to do in life, a long list indeed.

I crossed back to the north side of the city along Westminster Bridge and circled the tower of Big Ben. It welcomed me with a few good "bongs." I contemplated going into the Houses of Parliament, which were free, but the long lines put me off. Instead, I read the signs around the Jewel Tower and then headed for Westminster Abbey. For some reason it closes every Wednesday afternoon, which was just as well as my time was running short and I was soon to meet up with Tom.

I walked north up Whitehall until I got to Trafalgar Square and then turned west along Cockspur Street, turning once more at Regent Street. At Piccadilly Circus a newspaper seller directed me, rather rudely I might add (I'm sure he used his thumb), in the direction of the Royal Academy. Burlington House, which was our meeting place, actually serves as the quarters for the Royal Academy. My task would have been far easier had I realized this, as there are a lot of buildings named Burlington in this area. I spent some time in the Burlington Arcade, for example, before realizing that this could not be right. The main trouble was that there was scaffolding all around the facade of Burlington House and one had to just know it was there to enter. And if one didn't, well then, one didn't really belong there. This is after all the world famous Royal Academy, supporting such institutions as the Linnaean Society and the Royal Society of Antiquarians.

I got to our rendezvous point, which was the arch to the right upon entering, at 3:45 P.M., so I had a few moments to rest. After five hours of tromping about the city, I was starting to feel a bit tired. Tom emerged from the courtyard and warmly greeted me. He looked somewhat older than the last time I saw him fifteen years ago, but I of course have not changed one whit over the years. I was certain that he recognized me right off until he said, "You certainly look much different from your web site photo." Considering that picture was taken around 2000, maybe I have changed a wee bit. Oh well, we were in the Society of Antiquarians after all, so our visages were starting to fit in quite nicely.

Tom has been a member of this most prestigious of all archaeological societies for well over twenty years. Thus, he has access to the Library and could take a visitor into its extraordinary chambers. What a resource that library is. Just to be able to stand there falls beyond description. Unfortunately, Tom was not moved by my emotions. He, after all, had spent the day there and was anxious to depart. He grabbed his pack and off we went. Only when we were outside did he make mention of the portraits of past presidents on the walls, men like Sir Mortimer Wheeler and the like. "But of course you would have liked to see them. I should have pointed them out." Tom, like me, is a typical academic, not totally aware of surroundings when he is on a certain train of thought. And the objective of the moment was to find a pub, so that we did.

We rested for an hour over a pint of ale and became reacquainted. Tom and I have many interests in common and he is a delight to talk to. We ended up having some fish and chips at a pub near Euston Station and a coffee within the station itself. We vowed to stay in touch, which of course is much easier with e-mail. He gave me a picture of his "coronation" as Mayor of Kendal circa 2000 and asked that I pass it on to my Dad, which of course I will.

After saying our goodbyes, I headed off for Euston Square and took the Tube back to Liverpool Street Station. I really did keep to my goal of avoiding public transportation for all but the end of the day. Most people don't realize that feet really can carry one a great distance in a relatively short amount of time. Moreover, the landscape is far more interesting when viewed from street level. If destinations are the goal, then subways, buses, and taxis are the best devices of transportation, but as I have mentioned repeatedly in this narrative, the end points of routes are often incidental to the journey itself.

The Dedham Vale, Walking and Rowing with Constable

My objective for Thursday was to visit Dedham Vale, or rather "Constable Country," a landscape made famous by the early nineteenth-century artist John Constable, who also happens to be my favorite. I have always been amazed at how he not only captured the many details of country life and materials in his massive paintings, but he also caught the feel of life. As such, I wanted to see if the feel was still there in the land. It is not, for reasons I will get to.

Figure 49. John Constable attended this school in Dedham, Essex County.

But first I had to get to the Vale. Unwittingly, I had passed close by it several days ago in my return from Sutton Hoo. It is just off the A137 west of Manningtree, but to get to Dedham I had to turn on to the B1029 at Ardleigh Heath. I parked my car in the long-term lot between the town center and the old mill, a favorite in Constable's pictures, but long since gone. At around 10 A.M. I began my walk, first through the town past Constable's old school (Figure 49) and then down the path into the fields. At the first main juncture I turned right instead of taking the direct route into Flatford. This permitted me to see the countryside as it is now, rich in pasture, supporting herds of cattle as well as some sheep, and cultivated fields. Along the south bank of the Stour River, I walked the top of the levee, enjoying a scene rich in bird life. Canada geese, swans, and a host of ducks and other colorful maritime birds filled the scene (Figures 50 and 51).

When I got to the end of the line at Manningtree, I walked over the A137 bridge and had a bottle of lemon-limeade at the local petrol station. I asked directions of the proprietor as to how to get to a footpath on the northern side that would lead me to Flatford. He said what I had already feared, that there was none. It was certainly possible to head over the fields, but he took one look at my shoes and said, "That'd never do." Yes, I was embarrassed. I had already

Figure 50. *Horse and buggy riders in the Dedham Vale continue to provide a sense of "Constable Country."*

Figure 51. *Swans bathe and bask along the shore of the Stour River between Dedham and Manningtree.*

gone a mile into my walk when I realized that I hadn't changed out of shoes to hiking boots, so even though my wingtips were old, they definitely must have made me look strange. A Yankee accent and an Australian hat completed the ensemble. Several people had already mistaken me for an Aussie based on appearances alone.

I was not overly excited about retracing my steps, but there was no other choice (Figure 52). For a while it looked like the skies were going to open up, in concert with the incoming tide, but only a few drips came down—a good thing, too, as I was once again unprepared. I had anticipated sun and warmth all day and, for the most part, this is indeed what I got, but I did feel silly hiding beneath a bush for a while. When next I got to a Flatford turn, I took it, entering the complex from the rear of the mill, which is also depicted in many of Constables' scenes. I crossed the bridge and walked down the path to Willy Lott's house, central to the famous picture, "The Haywain" (Figures 53 and 54). Willy had lived there for all but four days of his eighty plus years of life, which I suppose is the essence of Constable's work, the stability of life. He depicted a way of life where people did not move much beyond their native hearth. What Thomas Hardy did with the pen, John Constable did with the brush, and that's exactly what is missing now, the correct people. Constable spent some time in

Figure 52. A turngate along the path back to Dedham.

Figure 53. Willy Lott's Cottage in Flatford is the subject of several of John Constable's paintings, including "The Haywain."

Figure 54. Constable's "The Haywain" shows Willy Lott's Cottage on the left.
(© National Gallery, London / Art Resource, NY)

Figure 55. Bovines along the Stour between Flatford and Dedham could have been drawn straight out of a Constable painting.

Figure 56. Waterfowl add to the pastoral scene.

the Lake District in his youth, but he did not like painting scenes there. Nature without folk was of no interest to him. As I look over the Dedham Vale now, I do see the same fields that he did, all largely untouched. There are also the descendants of the same cows and ducks (Figures 55 and 56), and the same kinds of trees and bushes. Even the houses and outbuildings are there that Constable saw on his daily walks, but what are gone are the people. Those who walk the streets now are truly aliens, visitors from both near and far who wish to relive a piece of the past when life was slower and simpler. I looked in vain for the horse-drawn cart in the river in front of Willy Lott's cottage and for the dog, which ran along the bank yapping at all the activity. No where is there life of the human sort, only ghosts of what was and will never be again. I suppose Constable himself realized this as he grew older, because less and less did he return to his native valley. The changes that he saw in a lifetime affected him as a painter. He himself began to move from realism to impressionism as he searched for the old thrills, the former emotions. And that's exactly what I miss about the Dedham Vale now, the emotions. As I rowed my boat (Figures 57 and 58) along the river between Flatford and Dedham, following the familiar turns in the course, all recognizable in Constable's landscapes, I realized that the landscape did not look all that different from a country scene in the States.

Figure 57. The bridge and teahouse at Flatford are main attractions for modern visitors.

Figure 58. The author rented a rowboat at the Flatford Bridge and set off along the enchanted waters of the Dedham Vale.

Constable brought his own emotions to the pictures he created and, in turn, we the modern visitors bring our sentiments. Without him the landscape is just a landscape, a pleasant day in the country to be sure, but not the same. When one reads Hardy, Thoreau, and Twain one relives a way of life that has long-since passed, but can still be recaptured by words. Constable and Rubens did the same with pictures. And to think that it's still possible to have such experiences while sitting on a sofa with a cup of tea and enjoying the quiet of home.

By the time I walked back to Dedham, it was already 5 P.M. I sat in the churchyard of St. Mary (Figure 59), another focal point of Constable's works, and wrote a dozen postcards. The way back to Colchester was pretty much without cars, as traffic had declined since "rush hour." Although it had declined, it had not disappeared. One cannot ride a road in England, at any time of the day, without having someone on your rear bumper. I don't know where they come from, as they just seem to appear miraculously, and the next time you look in your mirror they are gone. Cars make turns so quickly and without warning that driving is always an adventure.

I drove to The Fox Inn on the outskirts of West Mersea and had a wonderful meal of roast lamb shank, with the usual medley of vegetables (new potatoes,

Figure 59. The Church of St. Mary in Dedham occurs in a number of John Constable's works.

peas, carrots, and cauliflower). But this one was accompanied by a rich gravy and mint sauce, both very good. In fact, it was the best dinner I have had in England thus far. When I got back to Broman's Farm, I settled in the study and read about Constable and his life. What would life be without books? Probably just one speeding car after the other.

The Bower Hall Farm Red Hill on West Mersea Island

Today, May 27th is Avery's 22nd birthday. I asked Ruth if she would send an e-mail message to her and she was kind enough to do so. At 10 A.M. Ruth, Martin, and I went on an excursion to visit a Red Hill on West Mersea Island, just to the east of the causeway. We picked up Tess Sunnucks along the way, as she was to be our guide and permission. She lives in East Mersea Hall and for some reason has access to Maydays Farm, which borders on the site we were to go to. Her late husband James (he died two months ago) had a great love of the local prehistory and would have loved to be there, said Martin. I did note that he was a contributor to the Kay De Brisay Memorial Fund, as listed in the back of the *Red Hills of Essex* volume.

The site that we went to is called Bower Hall Farm (RH 86) (Figures 60 and 61). It is the property just to the west of Maydays. The Red Hill can still be seen as a large mass of bushes just beyond the seawall. We had a nice walk to it, admiring all the wild flowers and birds en route. Tess is a very vivacious sort, full of energy. She says she is in a depression through the loss of her husband, so I

Figure 60. Our initial approach to the Bower Hall Farm Site in West Mersea, as seen from the south.

Figure 61. The Bower Hall Farm Site (RH86) is really quite huge, as can be seen in this view looking southwest.

can't imagine how lively she would be if she felt good. She brought along her black Lab and he had a wonderful romp in the marsh. He wasn't overly friendly, but he did have his own agenda after all, and people just didn't fit into it.

I was amazed by the size of the site. The tallest part, the bulk of it, is set back from the edge of Pyefleet Channel. Despite the fact that it is surrounded by water at high tide, it is relatively immune to erosion (Figure 62). The beach, however, is slowly advancing and it won't be long before the little inlets totally enclose the hill, thus cutting off foot access. Remarkably enough, another coincidence, the site is depicted on the front cover of Fawn et al.'s *Red Hills of Essex* book. It is also represented by an 1896 sketch made by Henry Cole on the back cover. Because the pictures are of the edge of the site, the hill is not as dramatic as seen at the Tolleshunt d'Arcy site (RH 168) that I visited in the Goldhanger district. However, Cole (1906:173) reported a 2-foot-long 6-inch-wide trench on the extreme west edge of the hill, so the sites do share some parallels. It is so grown up now that my observations were confined to the beach. I had not intended to collect anything, but the recovery of two thin sherds, one of which was from a wheel-thrown vessel, could not be ignored. Cole had illustrated Roman sherds from this site in his 1906 study and Jefferies and Barford (1990) reported a Roman sherd in 1990 (circa A.D. 50–200), so I would imagine that

Figure 62. Ruth Dence, Tess Sunnucks, and Martin Dence pose at the Bower Hall Farm Site (RH86).

Figure 63. The two slots in the briquetage sherd from a hearth wall provide a clue as to usage. The potsherd on the left is from a wheel-thrown vessel.

this probably is one too. However, I need others to examine them.[20] Mrs. Sunnucks graciously donated the sherds to me and I, eventually, will give them to the Colchester Museum along with copies of fieldnotes and any other publications that follow.

Up until now I really didn't think that I would be able to contribute anything of significance with my research, but another discovery at Bower Hall has served as a form of "Rosetta Stone" for me. It is a medium-sized sherd that presumably broke from the upper wall of a clay-lined trench (Figure 63). What makes it so important is that there are two slots in it. I had suspected that firebars may have been spaced close together, as a result of examining one of the Goldhanger sherds at the Colchester Museum,[21] but here there could be no question as to the close spacing. Thus, the strength of the firebars seems to

---

[20] Further data on Bower Hall Farm come from Jefferies and Barford 1990:73-78. The sherds seen in Cole 1906 (Fig. 3 J-M) are said to be Roman from the picture, but they were not reexamined by Jefferies and Barford in their study. Of the six abraded sherds that they did report on, presumably from later surface collections, only one could be dated, a "Rough-cast beaker sherd, too small to assign form but date range could be A.D. 70-180." The authors assigned an overall date range for the site from A.D. 50-200.

[21] Which unfortunately is depicted upside down in Fawn et al. 1990:Fig. 18, right.

Figure 64. Close-up on a notch in the fireplace lintel in the dining room at Broman's Farm B&B, which helped me understand how firebars were used in salt production.

have come from being packed together, with just enough space between the bars for gas to seep out. The flues would have had to be fairly narrow, however, unlike the wide trenches of the hearths. Whereas pedestals supported the massive troughs to bring salt out of solution, I now believe that the firebars were involved in the salt drying process, which is a far gentler procedure. Inspired by the firebar–shaped hearth lintel that graces the Broman's Farm dining room, I am also now of the opinion that the firebar was used with its apex facing up (Figures 13 and 64). Already in the morning I had started writing about pedestals in my fieldbook, and now, because of this trip to Bowers' Farm, my thoughts on firebars had jelled. I looked forward to the afternoon when I could sit down and think with my pen.

We stayed at the site for perhaps an hour and then walked back to the car (Figure 65). Martin had retrieved a large board from the site, which made me chuckle. He reminded me of the industrious fellow that I had encountered on my Goldhanger walk, the one who happily discovered a wooden pole left by the tide. Could this just have been another coincidence of man appreciating resources and finding things to satisfy needs? Perhaps, but there have been many "coincidences" on this trip for me.

Figure 65. The Langenhoe District of Red Hills, as seen from the Bower Hall Farm Site (RH86).

When we returned to Mrs. Sunnucks' home, we found her 97–year–old mother hard at work in the garden and as happy as she could be. She is blind in one eye and stone-death, but mentally very sharp. She even sat with us in the garden sipping a glass of wine. What a marvelous large and old house this is. Martin told me it was the Manor house for the area and Tess said it is of 16th-century vintage. She was extremely angry about the pond, however, as it had been taken over by a red plant. They named it, with wrathful overtones, but all I really remember is that it was introduced from America! She was planning to bring in 600 pounds of weevils to consume the plants, but I rather imagine that could lead to other problems. Weevils, after all, have legs and can move out of ponds, can't they? Or perhaps I am getting out of my depth.

When we returned to Broman's Farm, I rearranged my pack and headed off to the Country Park at the end of Broman's Lane. There I sat at a picnic table for three hours or so thinking about salt making in Essex and trying to come to terms with how the various equipment and features were used. I ended up with a model of production, which fits with the data, but whether it is correct or not will perhaps never be known. However, the model has predictive value and can be tested by future archaeology.[22]

---

[22]   See Part III.

Figure 66. A pastoral scene along the Reeveshall Marsh in East Mersea.

It was 4:30 P.M. by the time I finished writing what turned out to be a 21–page essay. It was time for a walk, I decided, if only to clear my mind. I headed east from Cudmore Grove Country Park following the seawall and walked all along Pyefleet Channel as far as Maydays Marsh, almost within sight of the Bower Hall site, but not quite. I only half-heartedly looked for Red Hills, as I mainly wanted to have one last look at the Essex coastline (Figure 66). Birds to my right, cows to my left, and sheep straight on along my path, a fine mixture of surf and turf. Three hours later I finished up with my stroll and took life in hands by walking the road from Mersea Stone to the Dog and Pheasant Pub. On the last stretch of the seawall I was passed by a beautiful long-haired blond, who I only figured out later was "Paulina of Vancouver," the student I had met my first evening at the pub. Apparently, she and her girlfriend had given notice and were off in a week to Spain for the remainder of the summer. "Too quiet here?" I asked of her friend. "Yes," she whispered, "but don't tell." This change in plans must have just happened as the lady proprietor was in a very ill temper and kept going outside to harangue someone on the phone about "these exchange employees." I understand her plight, but she too should understand that these are 20–year–old kids who thought they had come abroad to see England. East Mersea does not really have youth much in mind. Now, if it's salt they are interested in, this is the place to be.

The Chiding Stone of Chiddingstone

On Saturday, May 28th I departed from Broman's Farm. I think the Dences were glad to be rid of me. Although I am an easy guest in that I pick up after myself and am quiet, they have had me for ten days, and a full breakfast for each of those mornings. I stretched those meals through most of the day and I'm sure Ruth wondered where I put it. Each morning I had a bowl of fruit of some sort, orange juice, a dish of porridge, and a hot plate that consisted of an egg, two links of sausages, two rashers of bacon, two grilled tomatoes, and mushrooms. Two slices of bread and a pot of tea completed the meal. If I ate like that at home I'd be 400 pounds, but then again I don't go out and walk for six hours at a stretch at home.

I was very directed this morning. My goal was to spend the day at the village of Chiddingstone (Figure 67). It is situated on the edge of the High Weald, with the River Eden flowing to its north. I was intrigued by its description in my guidebook, so that village became my target. I got there around 12:30 P.M. and today, just for a change, I decided to treat myself to a light lunch. I had leek and potato soup at a teahouse within the Burgesh Court, which has "A.D. 1453"

Figure 67. The burial ground of St. Mary the Virgin parish church in Chiddingstone, with a row of old buildings in the background.

Figure 68. The entryway to Burgesh Court in Chiddingstone.

boastfully written on its sign, but more of that later (Figure 68). The row of rickety timber frame buildings really is a delight, as is the church right across the street. I actually spent quite a bit of time on the church grounds photographing a number of the monuments. I suppose I could actually get interested in the English markers. They are not as boring as I thought from my last visit with Cabot. I was particularly intrigued by the epitaph, "Here lieth the body of…" instead of "Here lies the body of…" that we see in the States. There was also a fascinating stone, which had a cherub surmounted on a skull!

After walking around the village awhile, which I tried to stretch out as long as I could, I strolled down the path to the Chiding Stone (Figure 69), located on the southern edge of the "downtown area." I took a book along with me so that I could stretch out in the sun somewhere. It is fortunate that the sun was out, because there was a nip in the air. As might be expected, the village is named after the large unusually shaped sandstone outcrop located at the rear of the village… As chiding means scolding or condemning, it is supposed that this was a place where neighbors came to publicly air their grievances. In short, it was a seat of judgment. It is also thought to have been a Saxon land boundary, as well as a Druidic altar. People apparently were being chided here

Figure 69. The Chiding Stone in Chiddingstone is reminiscent of a giant mushroom.

Figure 70. The backside of the Chiding Stone can easily be mounted. Note the graffiti that adorns the surface of the rock, most of which is of twentieth-century vintage.

since at least A.D. 814, as that is the first written reference to the village. When the Domesday Book was written following the victory of William at Hastings (1066), Chiddingstone is known to have had both a church and the beginnings of a village street. According to the sign erected next to the stone, the row of houses dates to the sixteenth and seventeenth centuries, so the mid-fifteenth century date for the Burgesh Court appears to be wishful thinking.

There are writings, numbers, and signs carved into all parts of this unusual rock formation. The mushroom cap, which bears most of the writing, can easily be ascended along its northern exposure by using well-worn foot holes (Figure 70). You could just imagine a local muckety-muck climbing to the top of this stone, raising his arms, and passing sentence on some poor chide-ridden creature below. The land to the south of the stone rises gently, somewhat like an amphitheater. As I stood there on top of the stone, playing the role of the judge, I envisioned a mass of spectators, armed with pitchforks and the like, all anxiously awaiting my verdict.

The writings on the Chiding Stone are modern for the most part. The most recent inscription was added earlier in the month:

Regan
Hayden
Cerys
15-5-05

I saw another "Haydn," and although it is spelled differently, I suspect him to be an ancestral vandal. The earliest date that I saw was 1867, although there may also be an 1827, if I read it correctly. Most of the carvings are a late twentieth–century phenomenon, a product of my own lifetime, I'm embarrassed to say. Perhaps potentially dangerous places just do not instill fear or respect in us so much anymore.

I could not have found a better spot to read and relax. I chose a location on the southern side of the formation and discovered that the surface of the stone actually was quite comfortable. In fact, it fit the contours of my body perfectly. Under the heat of the sun, I started to doze, but that didn't last long. Soon after I closed my eyes the sky rapidly became overcast. The wind started to blow hard and cold, which was most uncomfortable. Plus, something must not have settled well with me from lunch, as I started to feel a pain in my belly. I eventually decided enough was enough and made a hasty retreat to the teahouse.

By the time I got out of the Gents' room the sun was shining once more as all the clouds had dissipated. I really hadn't thought about this rapid alteration in weather until now, as I am writing. Perhaps there really is something to tradition and sacred spots after all. Whatever the case, I don't believe I was particularly welcome beneath the Chiding Stone of Chiddingstone.

After having a nice drive through the East Sussex and Kent countryside, I got to Sunninglye Farmhouse around 5 P.M. I had a cup of tea with John and Suzie Petrie and visited with them and a couple of new guests from California. After reading some more in the Essex salt volume, I decided to give the Brown Trout pub in Lamberhurst another try. The last time I attempted to eat there it was on fire, and this time the power was out so they were limited as to what they could serve. When I asked the owner about the fire and told of my past visit, she said laughingly, "Maybe you ought not to come here again." Now I know what it means to be chided. Nevertheless, I did stay. The dressed crab salad and a jacket potato (baked) were very fine indeed—no belly aches.

Some Final Thoughts

I arrived home on Sunday, May 29. I had breakfast at 6:45 and was out of Sunninglye Farmhouse a half hour later. It was a little tricky finding the car rental drop-off at Gatwick, but I got there in such good time that a few ill-placed turns did not matter. Being a Sunday and a bankers' holiday at that meant there were only a few cars on the highways. I elected to take the M routes rather than the more direct A264. What I lost in mileage, I made up for in time and ease of mind. I had no trouble checking in my car, though they seemed to have a service fee for just about everything and by the time I'm finished the car is going to have cost me half as much again as what I budgeted. It's highway robbery, without the Dick Turpin, but what can you do? You really cannot make it around rural England without a car, so one must put up with the fiscal insults. God help me had there been a scratch anywhere!

I got into the terminal early and there was no problem getting checked in. I then did a leisurely stroll to my gate and settled down with the Essex Salt volume. I was determined to finish the book before quitting England and I came pretty close to meeting that goal, finally closing the covers midway across the Atlantic. It is such a fantastic volume, so concise, yet packed with incredible information and ideas, not to mention a bibliography that will keep me occupied for many years to come.

I tried to get a snooze on the plane, but had little success at that. A young English lad sat in the seat directly behind me and though he was "good as gold," he did have the table down for his various toys, workbooks, and the like, and he made good use of it. Any motion on his part soon made its way to me, so the trip was quite an amusement ride. But what could I do? He was just a young boy trying his best to be quiet and good. I gave up on trying to sleep and turned to Robert Louis Stevenson's *Inland Voyage*.[23] I have finished all but the Epilogue of that delightful travelogue. It was a most appropriate volume to read on my own peregrinations.

As we turned our nose down to Atlanta, the sky darkened. It had been raining over much of the South apparently, and though it was not a storm, it still was rather dismal. I made it through Customs with no problems and got to the baggage claim, but no Nancy. She turned up about five minutes later, having been delayed by all the rain and traffic. I was a bit concerned that my bag had gone astray within the airport, but it finally appeared and we were on our way.

Travel expands time, but long bouts of it can dull the senses. I have learned that two weeks on the road really is enough, and by the last day or two, no matter where you are, you're ready to come home, at least I am. I have also learned that B & Bs are the best way to go, at least in England. And the best formula is to stay in the first one for two nights in order to recover from jet lag, which is always worse going east. It is also good to return to that same B&B on the eve of departure, as it's a bit like returning to an old friend. I have also come to appreciate that ten days at the same B&B is just too much, even if you like it. Three to four nights per lodging is a good plan for future trips. That would give a mix of three to four B&Bs for a two-week journey. Cabot and I stayed at five two years ago and that was too much movement.

This trip to Essex, the focus of my stay, was far more productive research-wise than ever I imagined. The two days in the Colchester Museum examining box after box of briquetage was a key to the trip it turns out. It gave me an appreciation of the material that I could not get from pictures and text alone. Plus, I could see the problems for myself with regard to manufacture and use. Walking the landscape is critical. I spent three solid days on the seawalls familiarizing myself with both the land and sea where this great industry took place. And to have seen and surveyed two Red Hills that are still very much visible was a rare treat, especially as one had visible features.

---

[23] Stevenson 2004.

Even though so much of my time was devoted to research, I still saved time to explore and learn. I visited sites like Piltdown, Battle, and Sutton Hoo, and I toured cities like Colchester, Cambridge and London. These were lasting impressions, but I can say without hesitation that the villages are what intrigue me most. Dedham, Flatford, Thaxted, and Chiddingstone, all little communities, pretty at present and rich in tradition, these are the enduring charm of England.

Travel in the younger sort is a part of education; in the elder, a part of experience…It is a strange thing that in sea voyages, where there is nothing to be seen but sky and sea, men should make diaries, but in land-travel, wherein so much is to be observed, for the most part they omit it, as if chance were fitter to be registered than observation. Let diaries therefore be brought in use.

—"Of Travel" in The Essays or Counsels, Civil and Moral 1597–1625 *of Selected Writings* by Sir Francis Bacon 1982:48.

PART II
The Red Hills Explored

W hat follows is a review of publications that relate to the formation of the mysterious Red Hills of Essex and salt making. Although it now seems obvious that these massive mounds of red earth were the result of such an enterprise, this function was not so certain a century or so ago and it was heavily debated by some. And even when it was eventually determined that salt manufacture was the intent, there was little agreement as to just how it was produced. It took many years of archaeological investigation to solve the issue, but "solve" is perhaps an overstatement because there are many things that still do not add up. Contained in the Red Hills are the discards of an industry but, as suggested by the term discard, the vast majority of these objects have shifted from the location where salt was actually made, i.e. the hearth. Because these items are seldom found in place, reconstructing how they were used has not been an easy process. What I do in this section is take the reader on a chronological journey through the pertinent archaeological literature that helped me come up with a new model. I present the debate as it developed, but I should warn the reader that this is by no means a complete review of all that has been written about the Essex Red Hills. To take on that challenge would require a book at least double the size of the present volume. Rather, what I focus on in this section are specific contributions that made me rethink certain matters that just didn't seem to fit or that helped provide me with clues regarding the ground and the objects contained within. For those readers who find this approach a little tedious, I apologize beforehand and advise jumping to Part III for a synopsis, as represented by a new model of salt making in the Essex Red Hills. This model is based on personal observation of collections, considerable reading, and an even greater amount of manipulating my little gray cells, to quote a far more adept character than me in the solving of mysteries. It is to be noted that archaeology is a social science that builds upon that which has come before. Interpretations often are different, as new data appear, but credit is due to all those who wondered about the Red Hills in the past and presented their many thoughts as to what they might mean.

Stopes, H.
The Salting Mounds of Essex.
The Archaeological Journal 36: 369–372, 1879

This is a well-written, nice introduction to the Red-hills of Essex and offers excellent description. Stopes actually did dig some of the hills, with the main questions being what are the mounds, how did they come to be where they are, and who made them? He also is interested in when they were created and suspects that they date early. Stopes never does bring up the idea that they are related to salt production however. He makes mention of glass workers having come to Colchester in the thirteenth century A.D., but really does not think the Red Hills can be attributed to them. The mounds are consistently 2 to 4 1/2 feet thick he reports, and cover as much as 30 to 40 acres. Stopes also notes that Red Hills consistently occur in the tidal flats, never below them and seldom above. He describes the pottery as being coarse and having lots of fibers. He also mentions wedge-shaped objects that are well made and, from his description, sound as if they are firebars (Figure 71). He adds that they are seldom found whole, a characteristic that most later authors refer to also. Stopes describes the large vessels as well, all of which were fragmentary. In fact, everything in the Red Hills tends to be fragmentary, he says, which has been a major part of the problem in coming to terms with their function.

Figure 71. Five firebars from the Tollesbury site (RH 152), Tollesbury, Essex. All are of triangular form. Letter a has a pointed end, b and c have blunted ends, and d and e are mid-sections, missing their ends (Courtesy, Colchester Museum, Box label: "Tollesbury, 1977/78 K de B, F/BS & Peds, 1986.152.B10, CAG No. 152").

Atkinson, J. C.
Some Further Notes on the Salting Mounds of Essex.
The Archaeological Journal 37:196-199, 1880

This is a nice little study that builds upon the Stope 1879 contribution. The Rev. Atkinson had been aware of the Red Hills for over 50 years, as he chased rabbits on them as a boy, the loose soil having been perfect for burrows. He not only suggests that salt making was the function of these hills, but he presents the means for testing this idea. He argues first for the use of history and analogy. If salt actually was made along the Essex coast there should be a search for positive identification by virtue of documentary evidence. Also, there should be an accurate description of "salinae" elsewhere to draw from for comparisons. Drawing from *The History of Durham*, Atkinson discusses the Cowpen Marsh earthen mounds, which were known to have been a byproduct of salt manufacture. Salt had been made in Durham up to around 1580, and the mounds, he emphasizes, contains the same kinds of materials as the Essex Red Hills. Also, they occur on tidal flats, the same location as the Red Hills. All things considered, he feels that his hypothesis of salt manufacture in Essex is strengthened, and it certainly is. Then Atkinson considers the date of the Red Hills. This is difficult to get at, especially considering the lack of excavation, but he suggests that we might be able use linguistic evidence to establish when they were formed. If we were to look at place names, like "saltcote" for example, it can be seen that salt related names occur extensively in the coastal area. On this basis, Atkinson feels that the Red Hills date at least twelve hundred to thirteen hundred years ago. All in all, Atkinson's study is quite an impressive achievement for its time, in terms of both his logic and methods.

Reader, Francis W.
Report of the Red Hills Exploration Committee, 1906–7.
Proceedings of the Society of Antiquaries of London,
2nd Series 22: 165–181, 1908a

This is an excellent discussion of the work of the 1906–7 Red Hills Exploration Committee. They surveyed, mapped, and excavated numerous Red Hills in the Langenhoe and Goldhanger districts of Essex, with this report focusing mostly on the former. There is excellent description of the several excavations, with abundant section drawings (Figure 72). It was found that most of the hills

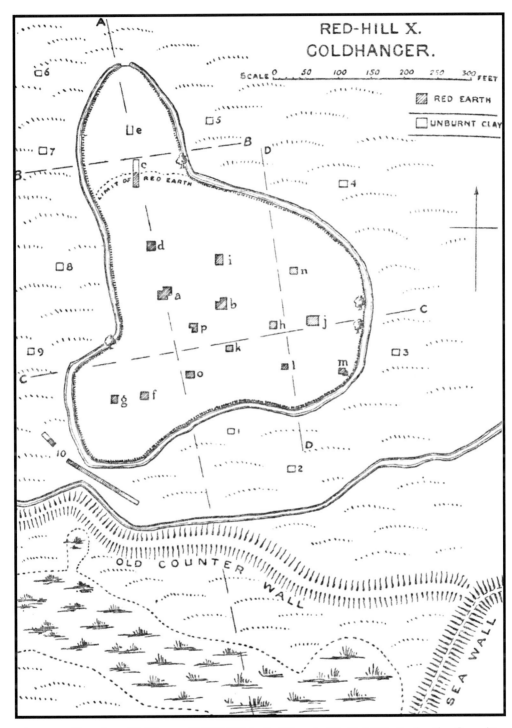

Figure 72. Plan view of Goldhanger X (RH 169) in the "Report of the Red Hills Exploration Committee 1906–7," as illustrated in Reader (1908a:Fig. 5).

went right down to the London Clay, but in some cases a carbonaceous layer of pressed plants was observed in between the clay and the red deposits. Very few features were seen in these investigations, the suggestion being that most parts of the sites were simply dumping grounds; that is, the garbage that resulted from work areas that occurred in a much smaller and limited space. Section drawings reveal that the surrounding ditches cut through the red earth, with the red soil continuing beyond their limits. Consequently, it is clear that the ditches are later features and unrelated to the activities that produced the red earth. This is a very important point. These hills continued to have an active life largely because they were hills and people were constantly shifting soil around to serve new needs. It is clear from the Red Hills Exploration Committee work that these later settlements may have nothing to do with salt manufacture, the more recent residents having simply used the spots because they are high and dry. Reader does believe that the Red Hills themselves are the result of salt making, but he emphasizes that their studies have not yet eliminated the possibility of pottery making. One thing that is certain, however, is that the activities that produced these hills are over by the end of the first century A.D.

Reader, Francis W.
Additional Remarks on the Pottery and Briquetage Found in the Red Hills of Essex, and Similar Objects from Other Localities. *Proceedings of the Society of Antiquaries of London,* 2nd Series 22: 190–207, 1908b

This work is supplemental to Reader 1908a but is supposed to be read in conjunction with it, if for no other reason than it contains almost all of the artifact illustrations that are referred to in Reader 1908a. The illustrations are excellent, truthful renditions of the artifacts, and I can say this because I myself saw just about all of the illustrated objects when I restudied the collection in the summer of 2005, courtesy of the Colchester Museum (Figures 73–75). The pottery section clearly reveals that the Red Hills continued to host occupation long after they first rose above the tidal flat landscape. Over and over they served as camps of some sort. The ditches were reamed out periodically to drain the raised areas and the Red Hill matrix was continually shifted about. Reader makes a valiant effort to come to terms with the artifacts that he now refers to

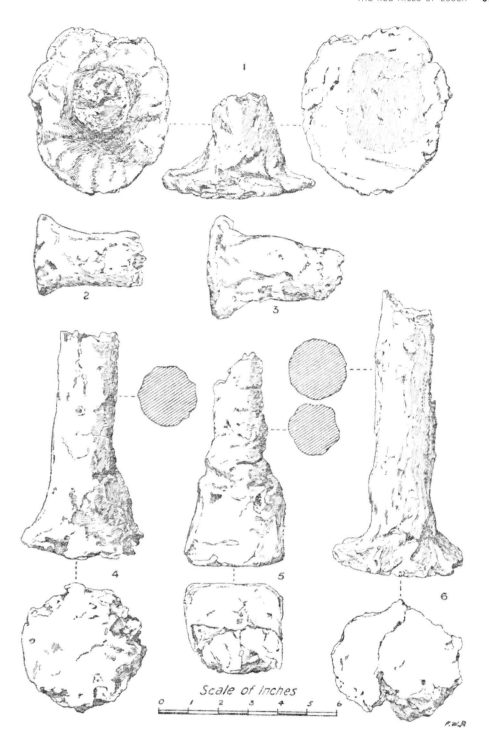

Figure 73. Fragments of pedestals from Goldhanger X (RH169), as illustrated in Reader (1908b:Fig. 13).

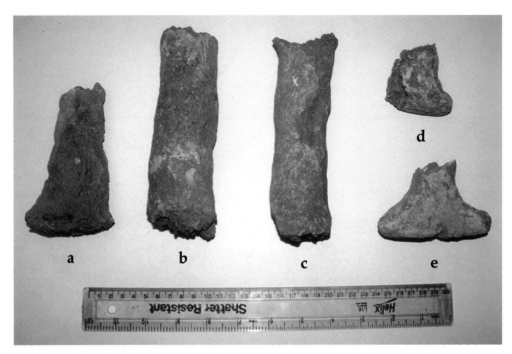

Figure 74. Five pedestal fragments and a "T-piece" (d) listed as briquetage from Goldhanger X (RH169) (Courtesy, Colchester Museum, Box label: No. 60, "Goldhanger, Redhill X, 1906, Firebars & Pedestals").

Figure 75. Base of a large pedestal found at Goldhanger X (RH169) (Courtesy, Colchester Museum, Box label: No. 196, "Red Hills, Briquetage, Goldhanger X." Bag Label: "PSAL 22, Fig. 13.1, Fig. 14.2").

as briquetage. Simply using the term is a reflection of his belief that the material is related to salt making, but he is not overly successful in demonstrating such, as he himself realizes. Reader does point out that there is a difference between the Langenhoe sites and Goldhanger X in that the former sites are rich in firebars while the latter are rich in pedestals. He does not know why this is so, but he feels it is significant enough to be mentioned. From the vantage point of a century of further archaeological work, it is more probable that these explorers had simply cut into different parts of a complex salt production system. If there really is a distinction between the sites, it is probably because of function rather than time or culture. One thing that this essay does reveal is a healthy reaching out to other areas for comparisons. Simply adopting the term briquetage is a move in this direction.

Reader, Francis W.
Report of the Red Hills Exploration Committee 1908–9.
Proceedings of the Society of Antiquaries of London,
2nd Series 23: 69–83, 1910a

This follow-up study represents the next stage of the Red Hills Exploration Committee's investigations, with excavations having been conducted at two sites in 1908. It is a relatively thorough site report for its time. The Goldhanger VIII site is the most thoroughly excavated of the Goldhanger district sites. It is here where prominent features were detected for the first time (Figure 76). Multiple flues were found that generally occur in sets of two. They run parallel to each other, have rounded ends, and are dug into the red earth. The latter observation is somewhat problematical, because it is not definite that the activities of the trenches, whatever they were, had actually produced the red earth. They seem to have been stages of a sequence. The underlying red earth, which is chock full of briquetage, could represent the dump, whereas the trenches are part of the work area, where the salt was actually made. These areas are characterized by heavily baked clay near the ends of the flues. It is reasonably clear that this must have been where the fires were lit, the heated air from such having been sucked into the flues. Clearly Goldhanger VIII was a very complicated site in 1908, and it remains so a century later. As of 2005, it supports an active sailing club and a concrete base support for an antiaircraft gun, a product of twentieth-century warfare (see Figure 17). The site experienced much usage over the years, from its initial birth as a Red Hill to its medieval

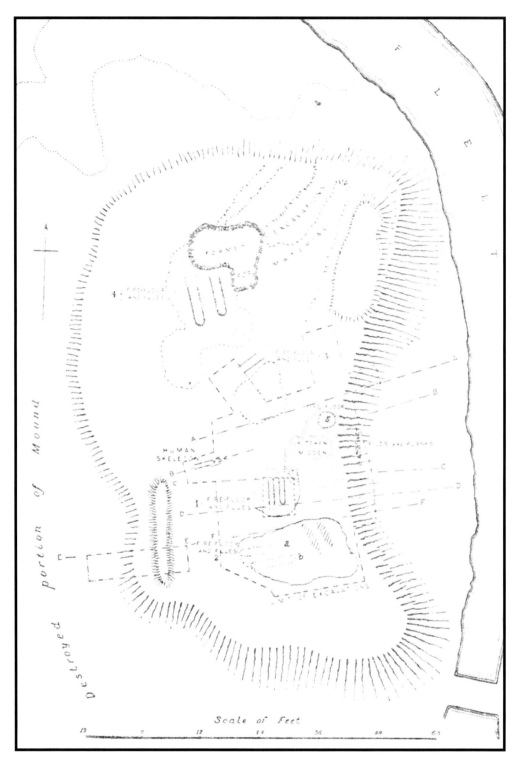

Figure 76. Excavations conducted on Goldhanger VIII (RH176). Note the sets of parallel flues (Reader 1910a:Fig. 4).

function as a fishery, to its modern employment for recreation. The last part of the Reader 1910a article is devoted to the Canewdon I site on the River Crouch. Observed here was a cluster of five red earth piles, which is what drew them to the site in the first place. For some reason they elected not to examine the area between the piles, an unfortunate circumstance because that might have been activity areas associated with salt making. The red earth at Canewdon I is recorded as being finer than elsewhere and more homogenous, probably because it contains lesser amounts of briquetage. The investigators note that shallow pits had been dug into the clay in the middle of the piles, features that are now recognized as evaporation tanks.

Reader, Francis W.
Notes on the Briquetage Found in 1908–9.
Proceedings of the Society of Antiquaries of London,
2nd Series 23: 86–88, 1910b

This is a much shorter report than Reader 1908b, but it reveals an increasing so-phistication in his understanding of the nature of briquetage. Some earlier mis-takes are corrected in this study, the most notable one relating to artifact type quantities. He highlights the fact that his previous study (Reader 1908b) gives the impression that pedestals, firebars, and other exotic objects are the most common briquetage found on Red Hills, but this is simply because of how fre-quently they are illustrated. In reality, says Reader, the "sagger-like chamber" is far more common on sites, and that clearly is the case at Goldhanger VIII and Canewdon I. We now know that Reader's "sagger-like chamber" refers either to portions of hearth walls or to trough[24] fragments, portion of vessels that were used for boiling brine (Figures 77 and 78), but Reader does not seem to have been aware of that in 1910. Consequently, he does not distinguish be-tween artifact (trough) and feature (hearth). Reader notes that there are far less pedestals, T-pieces, and firebars at Canewdon I for some reason, but again, that may be because of where on the site that they dug. A very important point is his reference to the marked similarity of the Goldhanger VIII and X site objects—"they appear to have been fashioned by the same hands in the same workshop (Reader 1910b:86)." I will return to this remarkable observation later.

---

[24] The term vat is used interchangeably with trough in the literature, but for consistency sake I use trough in this volume throughout.

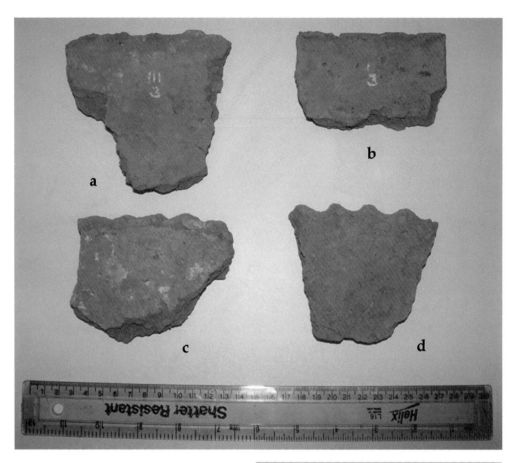

Figure 77. Examples of rim sections from four large troughs from Langenhoe III (RH89). Letters a, c, and d are scalloped and b has two lines in its lip (Courtesy, Colchester Museum, Box label: "CAG No. 89, 1986.37.B3" and "Red Hills Langenhoe III Briquetage." Bag Label: "Lang III, CAG 89" and "Langenhoe III 3."

Figure 78. Profile of trough rim sherd c in Figure 77. Langenhoe III (RH89) (Courtesy, Colchester Museum).

Petrie, William Flinders
Suggested Origin of the Red Hills.
Proceedings of the Society of Antiquaries of London,
2nd Series 23: 88–90, 1910

Petrie gives a nice summary of the byproducts of salt production at the commencement of his essay, but after that he presents only one idea as to how salt was made along the Essex coast. He is convinced that the salt was extracted from kelp burning and does not give much credence to the possibility that it could have been extracted directly from seawater. According to Petrie, marsh grass probably was the principal fuel involved. He reasons that because the slag is 2% of potash and rather less soda, this is "conclusive proof" for the vitrifying of the ash of marine plants or kelp (Figure 79). He then makes reference to several historical accounts of Celts having burned kelp along the Channel Islands and on the coast of France, which to Petrie is the denouement to the argument.[25]

---

[25] A recent report on the investigations at Stanford Wharf Nature Reserve in Essex revives the issue of using salt marsh plants in the local production of salt (Biddulph et al. 2012). Analyses of the Red Hill matrix at this site reveal it to be comprised mainly of fuel ash from the burning of salt marsh plants. Whereas traditional explanations of salt making in Essex involve the capture of seawater in reservoirs and its subsequent evaporation in troughs, Biddulph et al. argue that during the Middle Iron Age salt marsh plants would have been very common in the area. As compared to the ambient seawater, these plants would have had higher concentrations of salt in them. A two-stage process is envisioned where these plants were first harvested and burnt as fuel in order to evaporate brine in troughs. Then the resultant fuel ash would have been collected, rinsed in seawater, and filtered in order to increase the salt content in the brine that was stored in reservoirs. This makes sense, as the resulting brine produced by this process would indeed have a higher salt content than that normally found in the seawater. Moreover, any waste from the filtering process would have simply been dumped in the vicinity of the tanks, thus adding to the Red Hill formation. During the Roman period, however, there seems to have been an environmental change that affected the process, because marine plant roots and rhizomes are rare in the region at this time. Because there would have been little sediment adhering to the plants used in the burning process, salt makers of the Roman period who were in need of fuel would have resorted to harvesting bits of vegetation above the sea floor or gathering plants on the ground instead of yanking the salt marsh plants out of the mud. And because mud was no longer adhering to the plants used in the process, there would be no significant increments to the Red Hills when the plants were burned (Biddulph et al. 2012:79-81, 164). I am indebted to Paul R. Sealey for bringing this valuable work to my attention.

Figure 79. Large chunk of slag with vitreous glass-like drippings on the inside of a hearth from Gold-hanger X (RH169) (Courtesy, Colchester Museum, Box label: No. 198, "Red Hills, Goldhanger, X 1906, Vitreous Slag &, Burnt Earth").

Jenkins, J. H. B.
Remarks on Dr. Flinders Petrie's Theory.
Proceedings of the Society of Antiquaries of London,
2nd Series 23: 90-96, 1910

Jenkins is not at all enamored by Petrie's theory of kelp burning. First he attacks the data itself, arguing that the alkali in the slag that Petrie mentions is mostly soda, not potash, and that would most likely come from the boiling of seawater, not plants. In addition, using an environmental perspective, Jenkins argues that the low-lying gentle coast of Essex is not at all attractive to the growth of kelp, which elsewhere in the world prefers a rocky shore. In short, Petrie's theory does not stand up to the evidence.

Smith, Reginald A.
(The Essex Red Hills as Saltworks).
Proceedings of the Society of Antiquaries of London,
2nd Series 30: 36–53, 1918

Eight years after the Red Hills Committee's investigations came to a close, Reginald Smith reexamines the old data and presents some new thoughts. He first provides a thorough review of the past literature in his essay, including references to Cope, Atkinson, and the various Reader studies. He goes on from there to stress that briquetage found on the continent is an important source of information that has not yet been given appropriate attention. To be fair, however, Reader (1908b) does adopt the term briquetage, so that in itself implies that he saw correlations with salt making on the mainland. What Smith does is expand the study by drawing from finds in France and Germany. He believes that salt could have been made by first stacking the briquetage in a rather complex scaffold-like arrangement. Brine was subsequently dripped on to the scaffold and, as it filtered down through the intricate web, salt crystals began to form. Once the clay objects were covered with crystals and the evaporation process came to an end, the scaffolding would have been dissembled and scraped. Although certainly possible, what a labor-intensive project this would have been. That it could have occurred is supported by the Roman observation of Celts having dripped brine on to burning wood.

Wilmer, [Horace]
(Comments on "The Essex Red Hills as Saltworks" by Reginald
A. Smith). *Proceedings of the Society of Antiquaries of London,*
2nd Series 30: 53-54, 1918

In his reaction to Smith's 1918 paper, Wilmer emphasizes that the interior salines of Europe are not necessarily a good form of comparison for the Essex Red Hills situation. Because the Seille Springs in Germany are 33% saturated with salt, pure sodium chloride would have quickly resulted from pouring its brine over heated bars. Seawater, on the other hand, is only about 3% saturated with salt, so it would take an inordinate amount of briquetage and labor for the scaffold procedure to have been adopted in a coastal environment. It quite simply would not have been economical along the Essex shoreline. Moreover, the mushroom-like pedestal is the only form of Essex briquetage that Smith incorporates in his recreation of the process. The firebar, which Wilmer calls the "furnace bar," does not even enter into the equation. Nor does Smith involve flues in the process, despite the fact that they are found in significant numbers at several of the sites investigated by the Red Hills Committee, especially at Goldhanger VIII (see Figure 76). Wilmer's commentary ends with a somewhat disturbing statement, considering all the time and effort that had already been devoted to solving the Essex Red Hills mystery:

> The salt-theory had been brought forward on several occasions, and every one recognized in it a possible solution of the problem. Both the number and nature of the mounds implied the former existence of an organized industry. In his own opinion the production of salt was the only explanation, but the late Dr. Laver would not accept the theory without convincing evidence; and it was not clear how the red earth contributed to the production of salt. He [Wilmer] felt that though the Society was indebted to the author for further information on the subject, it had not yet been proved how salt was manufactured on the Red Hills.
>
> —Wilmer 1918:53-54

Riehm, Karl
Prehistoric Salt–boiling.
Antiquity 35 (139): 181–191, 1961

It would be more than four decades before another scholar offered new data to address the issue. In 1961 Karl Riehm published his "Prehistoric Salt–boiling" article with the Essex Red Hills problem in mind, and he too draws from findings on the continent for analogies, especially from Germany (the Halle saline) and France. He first summarizes the early work of Reader et al., and commiserates with their frustration. The new discoveries of briquetage at Halle allows him to look at the Red Hills from a different perspective. He recognizes a four-stage evolution in pedestals at Halle that starts with a single goblet shape and ends with a two-part implement of a cup (or auget) supported by a pillar (Figure 80). In essence, Riehm believes these objects were a currency of sorts and that the evolution of the pedestal led to standard-sized vessels that could be shipped far and wide. According to Riehm, these objects began to

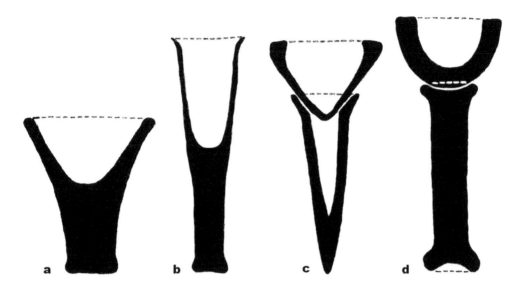

Figure 80. Evolution of pedestals/augets at Halle in Germany. A, Goblet; b, Narrow Chalice; c, Hollow Cone on Quiver; d, Jar on Cylindrical Pillar (Adapted from Riehm 1961:Fig. 1).

Figure 81. Two augets of the same form from Loire Atlantique, France (Courtesy, Colchester Museum, Box label: "Briquetage, De Brisay Collection, Loire Atlantique, 2000.179.B4").

appear in the archaeological record at Halle around 1000 B.C. during the Late Bronze Age. Although small porous bowls or cups, referred to as augets in France, have been recognized in England, they are rare, especially in Southeast England. I myself am not yet convinced that they ever figured much in the production and distribution of salt along the Essex coast, primarily because I did not see anything that looks even remotely like an auget in the Colchester Museum collections. It is interesting that De Brisay did collect some of these objects in at least one of her travels, however, because there are some extremely nice thin-walled augets from the French coast in the comparative collections at the Colchester Museum (Figure 81).

After discussing the German finds, Riehm then proposes a very complex reconstruction of a salt-boiling oven at Ingoldmells in Lincolnshire. He suggests that the prehistoric salt-makers at Ingoldmells may have scraped up a mixture of sand and salt from solar pans and then burned it, thus producing the red earth. As sand scraping and burning have been observed ethnographically in Africa, it certainly is a possibility. Although one cannot eliminate the possibility of such, as there surely are many different ways to make salt, it seems to me that it would not be very economical as too much fuel would be required. Moreover, the process really does not match well with the archaeological features in Essex.

Tessier, Michel
The Protohistoric Salt Making Sites of the Pays de Retz, France.
In *Salt, the Study of an Ancient Industry*,
edited by K. W. De Brisay and K. A. Evans, pp. 52–56.
Colchester Archaeological Group, Colchester, 1975

It is worthwhile taking a closer look at the European data, because discoveries made in France and Germany in the 1960s definitely had an impact on how Kay De Brisay and others ended up evaluating their finds when excavations started up again in Essex in the 1970s. One study that had an impact was Michel Tessier's work at coastal briquetage sites located at or near the mouth of the Loire River. This article reads like conference notes in the De Brisay and Evans' edited volume, *Salt, the Study of an Ancient Industry*. The presumed ovens that he describes seem a bit fanciful, especially the so-called "gratings," but he does illustrate a very interesting pit that is roofed over with rock slabs.

Clay pedestals support the roofing material itself. Although it is hard to tell from the drawing, it seems as if the pedestals either protrude through the slabs or that cups are set on top of the rock. It is unclear from the article whether or not such an intact structure was actually found or whether the illustration is simply a reconstruction for the sake of discussion. One long oven that Tessier describes fits well with hearths of the enclosed type observed in Essex. It is a narrow ditch, about 4 m long, .45 m wide, and .5 m deep, and is shown having stones spanning the top. These stones apparently are the equivalent of the clay firebars found in Essex. The artifact descriptions in this article are very useful for comparative purposes. It is interesting that the thin-walled auget that Tessier describes has sides that are slightly concave.[26] Interestingly, Tessier refers to having found a stack of these augets, which is reminiscent of stacks of pointed base cups observed at the sites of Shaopengzui and Wazhadi sites in Zhong Xian, Sichuan Province, China (Brown 2006:Fig. 2; Flad 2004:346, Fig. 5.25). In an end note to Tessier's study, Warwick Rodwell says that the green glassy slag that occurs on the outside of the Essex containers (see Figure 79) had to have resulted from "enormously hot fires," the kind of heat that one would expect from enclosed ovens, although Rodwell does not actually say that. Nevertheless, his observation is important.

Kleinmann, Dorothée
The Salt Springs of the Saale Valley.
In *Salt, the Study of an Ancient Industry*,
edited by K. W. De Brisay and K. A. Evans, pp. 45–46.
Colchester Archaeological Group, Colchester, 1975

In this article Kleinmann offers more detail on the evolution of pedestal–augets in the Salle Valley (Halle) of central Germany, picking up where Karl Riehm (1961) left off. In terms of the history of archaeology, it is of some interest to note that Riehm's fascination with pedestal–auget evolution probably came about as a result of finding them in his own backyard in great quantities. A 1-meter-thick archaeological stratum provided him with the sequence order and Kleinmann is able to offer a refinement of dates in her article. Although

---

[26] This attribute also occurred on the augets that De Brisay collected and deposited in the Colchester Museum collections (see Figure 81).

salt making has been traced back to the Early Bronze Age at Halle at around 1800 B.C., it is important to note that only basins and oval pillars were used at that time. The pedestal–auget evolution that both she and Riehm discuss began at around 1000 B.C. and ended during the Hallstatt period of the Iron Age circa 400 B.C. This would suggest that the use of salt as currency, if this is what augets actually indicate, is a Late Bronze Age to Iron Age phenomenon in central Germany. Kleinmann is puzzled as to just why augets are found so far removed from salt springs, but I do not find this curious at all. If salt actually were used as currency during the last millennium B.C., it probably would have been transported in these small clay containers (Morris 1985; 1994). Consequently, it would be far more surprising to find vast quantities of augets where the salt was produced. An exception to this might be augets that are damaged, as they presumably would have been discarded at the salines. Once again, I think it is important to highlight that the absence of whole or fragmentary augets in the Red Hills of Essex implies that salt may never have been used as currency there, but the verdict is still be out on that matter.

De Brisay, Kay
Preliminary Report on the Exploration of the Red Hill at Osea Road, Maldon, Essex. *Colchester Archaeological Group Bulletin* 15:23-43, 1972

The 1970s represents a period of resurgence in the Red Hills of Essex. The ringleader in this new attack on the problem was Kay De Brisay of the Colchester Archaeological Group. Her first major contribution was the excavation of the Osea Road site in the Goldhanger District. This site, listed as No. I in the Red Hills Exploration Committee work (Reader 1910a), is located along the east edge of the causeway road that leads to Osea Island. A caravan park is currently situated immediately west of the site and the site itself is in pasture. The initial season of work at the site in 1971 represents the first modern excavation of a Red Hill, as well over half a century had passed since the Red Hills Exploration Committee completed their explorations. Four trenches were dug out from a central point (CP) at Osea Road, which also happened to be its highest point. The trenches were dug at right angles using heavy machinery and each of the walls revealed a remarkable amount of discrete angled layers, or "tipping".[27] For the most part these layers dipped inland towards the CP, but it is important to note that whenever dense work areas were encountered, such as at the "Southern group" and at the CP, the tipping tended to radiate out from these spots. This makes sense with regard to dumping activities. If the ancient salt workers discarded waste in a regular fashion, it is logical that they would have carted the debris to the edge of a growing platform. And if economy of labor were an issue, the platform itself would have grown in essentially a circular fashion. De Brisay observed a series of evaporation tanks, normally in sets of three, in both the Northern Group and the Southern Group of her excavations. These features are believed to have held brine over the course of a summer and were topped off periodically as the water evaporated. In short, by taking advantage of natural agencies, the sun and prevailing wind, the brine would have become increasingly concentrated. Eventually a gentle heat from an artificial source was all that was needed to bring salt out of solution.

The excavators at Osea Road found a whole pedestal, which is a very unique find as they are almost always found in a fragmentary state. This complete pedestal revealed once and for all that the so-called "T-Piece" (Reader 1910a:178; 1910b) is not a distinct artifact (see Figures 74d). Rather, it now could be demonstrated that it was one end of a cylindrical pedestal, the other end flaring into a mushroom shaped base. To be sure, this is something that was not totally unexpected, but until a complete pedestal came to light proof was lacking. De Brisay notes that for the Osea Road pedestals the longer part of the stem generally stays with the head. I did not notice this to be the case when I examined the briquetage collections at the Colchester Museum however. Similar to what Reader indicates (1908a:178), more often than not the many pedestals that I saw in the museum collections have the greater portion of their stems attached to their bases, not their tops; this is important, as we shall see. Firebars are described for Osea Road, but as they were not observed in context, De Brisay is unable to say much more than earlier investigators about their function.

One discovery of the Osea Road excavations, which merits highlighting, is the in situ placement of sockets. These circular depressions mark where pedestals were shoved into a working clay surface. These are considered to be the lo-

---

[27] Tipping relates to the disposal process and can be recognized easily in stratigraphic sections. Reader describes the process in his report on the Langenhoe Red Hill I (RH 95) excavations, "The briquetage was found not only scattered throughout the red soil, but occurred in occasional patches, as did also some unburnt clay and wood ashes. These in the sections mostly showed in curved seams, and the whole had the appearance of soil that had been 'tipped,' being in a successive series of hummocks (Reader 1908a:170."

*Figure 82.   Hearth fragments bearing wattling impressions from Osea Road, Goldhanger I (RH184)
(Courtesy, Colchester Museum, Box label: "Osea Road, Wattling, CAG 184, 1986.117.B4").*

cation of open hearths, because trenches were not identified. However, the fact
that De Brisay's refers to wattling on some of the troughs I find curious (Figure
82). One wonders if she may not be describing the walls of a hearth and, if so,
there is then the implication that a closed oven was located nearby.

De Brisay, Kay
A Further Report on the Excavation of the Red Hill at Osea Road, Maldon, Essex. 1972. *Colchester Archaeological Group Bulletin* 16:19-38, 1973

De Brisay continued her excavation of the Osea Road site during an eight-week period in the summer of 1972. The excavators laid out a 30-meter square to the north of Trench D, adjacent to where the three evaporation tanks of the Southern Group were found in the previous year. The outer edges of this large square were excavated, thus revealing another three-tank set nearby. Farther to the north a more complex network of evaporation tanks were detected that consisted of at least six tanks. A ditch that ran through a portion of the square is believed to be evidence of later usage of the site. From aerial photos it can be seen that the Osea Road Red Hill covers a natural drainage pattern that is no longer extant. The presence of evaporation tanks is consistent with this observation, because tidal waters would have run up to the site during occupation. As with the first season, section drawings reveal that tipping radiates out from the work areas.

Some additional complete pedestals were found during the second season at Osea Road, but the clay floors yielded no more sockets. From an analysis of site strata, De Brisay came up with a sequence of firebar forms. She argued at the time[28] that flat-topped heavy construction occurred first (Phase I), followed by flat-topped light construction (Phase II), and finally by the pointed top form (Phase III). The investigators also recovered shards from the walls of large, rectangular troughs. The shards are either flat or gently curved and some of them could be pieced together, with enough joints to determine vessel shape. De Brisay says that there is folding and joining of clay at the corners of these vessels, which, as we shall see, is a very important observation. She also detected wattling impressions on the bases of these troughs, as well as grain impressions. A white deposit is also seen on the surfaces of several shards. These troughs, she says, would have been so heavy, especially when filled with brine, that the pedestals would have be set solidly in the ground in order to support them.

---

[28]   De Brisay's later excavations at the Peldon site would convince her that she had initially reversed the sequence.

De Brisay, Kay
The Excavation of a Red Hill at Peldon, Essex: Report on the First Year. *Colchester Archaeological Group Bulletin* 17:25-42, 1974

De Brisay's later work at the Peldon site (RH117) was a challenge, to say the least. The site itself occurs just to the south of the Peldon Rose, a widely acclaimed pub. I myself can vouch for its quality and good cheer (see p. 45). Mrs. K. A. Evans was the owner of the Peldon site at the time it was excavated, revealing a clear personal interest between the Evans' family and Red Hills research.[29] Initially the excavators of the Peldon site placed their units on dry land, but they soon discovered that the heart of the site lay beyond the seawall. This posed a whole new problem. Excavations were difficult because for at least three hours every twelve hours the site was inaccessible because of tidal waters. They did dig a drain, which helped somewhat, but any site that is flooded twice a day is bound to lose some integrity. Moreover, the work itself was still a very messy endeavor.

A similarity between Peldon and Osea Road was the discovery of multiple evaporation tanks (Figure 83). There are at least three in a row at Peldon and there may actually have been more. One welcome addition at Peldon is the appearance of a well-defined hearth located next to the tanks. Fired clay walls are believed to have once enclosed the hearth. Fragments of the walls had finger grooves running vertically in their inside and some of the tops of these wall sections bear firebar impressions. From the drawing that is offered (De Brisay

---

[29] This harkens back to Karl Riehm's own interest in briquetage, which may have been stimulated, though I do not know this for sure, from this material having been found in such great quantities in his backyard. One consistent aspect of the Essex Red Hills research is that the local gentry have always been the prime catalysts for investigations. With the exception of specialty topics, most of the excavators and reporters of Red Hill findings in Essex are denizens of the county. This has certain advantages, because local folk have a vested interest in the history of their land, but there is also a disadvantage. It seems to me that Red Hills research has occurred in spurts largely because the people who conduct it are either retired or rapidly approaching this status when they begin their studies. With all due apologies to those who are young at heart, it is a sad fact that very few of the Essex Red Hill investigators have had the time or resources during their most productive years to give to archaeology. Professional archaeologists seldom have Red Hills explorations as a prime research endeavor, with Sealey's 1995 work being an important exception. As "Father Time" catches up with everyone eventually, few students of the Red Hills have been able to devote more than a decade or so to their research.

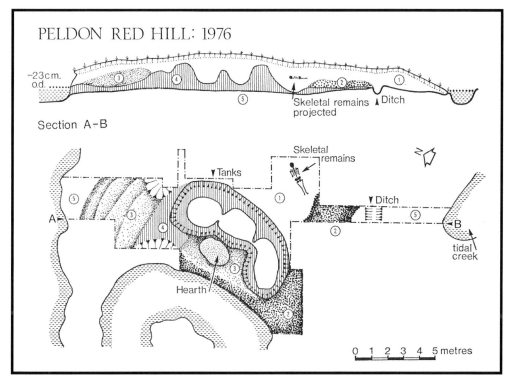

Figure 83. Plan and section of Peldon (RH117) showing three evaporation tanks, a hearth, and evidence of tipping (De Brisay 1978a:Fig. 2). By permission of the Society of Antiquaries of London.

1974:Figure 1), however, the firebar would have to be used with its pointed side facing up, though De Brisay does not say that was so. There are lots of firebars at the Peldon site, but pedestals are lacking. Their total absence (at least at the time this particular article was written) really is extraordinary, but Reader (1910b:88) does indicate that there are indeed significant differences in the briquetage found at various sites. The immediate suggestion is that different salt production processes were employed at Osea Road and Peldon, but it is also possible that the variations relate to functional differences, which I shall return to below.

The vessel shards found at Peldon are of two basic forms: trough-shaped and circular. De Brisay reevaluates the firebar sequence as a result of the Peldon finds and comes up with a different sequence. Whereas all three forms (flat-topped heavy construction, flat-topped light, and pointed top) are found at Osea Road, only the pointed top form is recovered at Peldon. Because only Belgic pottery (1st century B.C.) was found at Peldon, whereas Belgic and Roman pottery appear at Osea Road, De Brisay reasons that the pointed top form must be the earlier. I do understand the logic behind her reasoning, but the implication of such is that the strata upon which the initial Peldon firebar sequence was established (see p. 103) must have been inverted. That may indeed be true, but because of the indirect nature of the reasoning, it makes me question whether a sequence really exists at all. At this point, I do not think the directionality of a sequence can be convincingly defended, one way or the other.

De Brisay, Kay W.
The Red Hills of Essex. In *Salt, the Study of an Ancient Industry*, edited by K. W. De Brisay and K. A. Evans, pp. 5–11. Colchester Archaeological Group, Colchester, 1975

This article is a summary of the Essex salt production processes, as of 1975, by virtue of De Brisay's major excavations at the Osea Road and Peldon sites. Even though the sites are not that far apart, the artifacts and features are different. De Brisay believes the differences are due to the operations having been small family-level enterprises. In essence, the variations are thought to be the result of people doing things just a little differently from others. She describes numerous features in this study, including working floors, hearths, and evaporation tanks, with the latter always occurring in sets of three. Although a case can certainly be made for these sets, the detailed excavation drawings in her various reports suggest to me that there may have been more tanks at some of the work areas at both Peldon and Osea Road. Once again, she highlights the occurrence of two pedestal sockets in one of the clay floors at Osea Road and also mentions that a complete pedestal was found there, thus eliminating the notion of the T-Piece as an artifact type. I agree that such objects were once part of the complete pedestal form, but I am not so sure that we should dismiss the importance of the T-Piece. There may be a reason relating to the construction of the hearths as to why pedestals are so seldom found whole, a point I will return to in Part III of this study.

De Brisay mentions in her essay that firebars have never been found in place, but this time she emphasizes that the clay lining of a trench wall at Peldon reveals that firebars once rested on top of it. At Peldon the firebars would have been used with a closed hearth, says De Brisay. On the other hand, at Osea Road pedestals would have supported firebars over an open hearth, with the points of the firebars facing down. From what I have been able to find, there is no direct evidence from Osea Road, or any other site for that matter, that proves this orientation. In fact, the Peldon data would seem to make a better case for firebar points having faced up when they were in use.

Jones, M. U.
Prehistoric Salt Equipment from a Pit at Mucking, Essex.
The Antiquaries Journal 57 (Pt. 2): 317–319, 1977

This study by Jones is very important, I believe, because it relates to briquetage that was recovered over 2 km distant from the nearest source of salt. The objects in question are found in association with pits that are thought to have stored clay. The briquetage itself consists of bits and pieces of fired clay. The two forms that he illustrates are of some interest. One object is a cylindrical tube with a cupped end, which does indeed resemble a pedestal, while another object is an L-shaped slab that looks like a trough section. Jones interprets these artifacts to be the remnants of salt-making equipment that was made on location, eventually to be taken to places where it would be used. For some reason, though, these particular objects never left the site. Other pits near the one that he describes also contain clay scraps of briquetage, so this is not an isolated find. Jones notes that Kleinmann (1975) observed a similar situation at Halle in Germany, wherein briquetage occasionally turns up on sites distant from salt sources. Jones then makes what I believe to be a very profound observation. He reasons that if salt making along the coast was a seasonal activity, it would be logical for some of the briquetage to have been made in advance, and that could most easily have been done at a home base.

De Brisay, Kay
The Excavation of a Red Hill at Peldon, Essex, with Notes on Some Other Sites. *The Antiquaries Journal* 58 (Pt. 1):31-60, 1978a

I believe this article is the best of De Brisay's studies in that she not only presents the final report of the important Peldon site using excellent graphics, but she also compares it to Osea Road and other sites in Essex, and in England overall. The final Peldon site report really does not differ all that much from her preliminary study, but it is a far better summary. By now De Brisay has got it settled in her mind as to how salt production was done in Essex (Figure 84). To her, firebars are the key to the operation, as they are the principal supports for two different trough forms. They are either used in conjunction with pedestals on an open hearth, or they are the sole support, having been set in trenches of closed hearths. The trouble with this formulation is that by the time of De Brisay's final report pedestals were starting to make an appearance at Peldon. They certainly do not occur as frequently as firebars, but they definitely are there. How then do they relate to the closed hearths at Peldon, or do they? Unfortunately, De Brisay does not address this question. She does, however, get into some discussion in this particular article about the manufacture of briquetage. She argues that the various objects, including pedestals, firebars and troughs, were made using a bonfire technique. Although this is certainly possible, what seems strange to me is if the briquetage was being fashioned on site, no matter whether in a kiln or not, why does it often occur with a wide range of tempers? Grains are commonly used as temper, De Brisay says, but in addition to grain impressions I myself have also seen crushed flint and chalk (Figures 85 and 86).

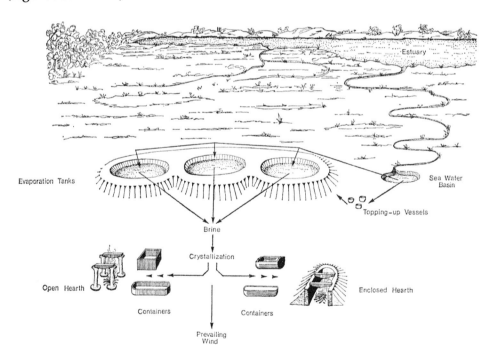

Figure 84. De Brisay's suggested sequence for the operation of a Red Hill, with one variation being an open fire and the other a closed hearth (De Brisay 1978a:Fig. 4). By permission of the Society of Antiquaries of London.

Figure 85. Trough fragment from Goldhanger X (RH169). Burned vegetable matter occurs on what is presumably the inside of the trough. The impressions of seeds are still clearly visible. Also, the inside and outside of the container have wide bands of smoothing that run parallel to the top of the trough (Courtesy, Colchester Museum, Box label: No. 113, "Red Hills, Goldhanger, X Troughs").

Figure 86. Pedestal stem and base from Goldhanger X (RH169). The object has large chunks of chalk as temper, which is not an Essex feature. It seems to have been formed by rolling a large wad of coarse clay over a marled surface, probably wood, as the exterior of the cylinder has a wooden board-like surface with striations running vertically. The base is reduced up to about 4 cm along the shaft, the rest of the pedestal being oxidized. There are no discolorations on the bottom of the base (Courtesy, Colchester Museum, Box label: No. 90, "Goldhanger, Redhill X, 1906, Firebars & Pedestals").

I find it most interesting that grains are used so frequently, because they would have been available only after threshing, which occurs at harvest time. De Brisay does make note of this in her article, but if the briquetage is being made on site, the implication is that the salt producers would have stored the grain over the winter and then brought it out to the Red Hills to roll with the clay into dough. Although that certainly may have happened, all that can really be said is that the grain was available only following threshing. In other words, briquetage could have been made at any time between when the harvest occurred and when the artifacts had their final employment on a Red Hill site during the summer months.

De Brisay, Kay
The Red Hill at Tollesbury, Essex: Final Report.
Colchester Archaeological Group Bulletin **22:2-8, 1979**

Although this represents the final report on the Tollesbury Red Hill (RH152), it really needs to be read in conjunction with the preliminary report (De Brisay 1978b), which has much information in it that is not covered here. The Tollesbury site is located just inside the sea wall, but it is so difficult to access that the excavators were only able to dig a single trench through the site. A section drawing and a plan view are the main visual contributions, but other than a work area on the western end of the trench, there is little else to offer with regard to features. The artifacts, however, are of some interest. First off is the discovery of an auget at Tollesbury, which if that is what it really is, is the first report of such that I have encountered for Essex. Whereas pedestals dominate at Osea Road and firebars are predominant at Peldon, at the Tollesbury site these objects occur with basically equal frequency. Could this be because they were used in different contexts in the salt production technology? De Brisay does not really consider this question, but it is an important one to keep in mind because function may affect distribution.

Something that is also interesting is De Brisay's observation that the firebars at Tollesbury are very carefully made, as compared to the pedestals. Moreover, the pedestals vary considerably in form. Although they all are broken, it is clear that they originally had different tops and bases. To me this suggests different makers may have been involved, but are we looking at differences that occur over time or are the variations the result of the same hearths having different pedestals within them? It is impossible to address this question

Figure 87. Five pedestals from Sawdons Marsh, Peldon IX (RH106). Letter a is a base with a rectangular cross-section and slightly concave walls. The base plugged into a platform of sorts or was in the ground, as glazing stops about 5.3 cm above the bottom of the pedestal. Letter b is reportedly rectangular, but its cross-section is actually a parallelogram. Letters c and d are mid-sections of cylindrical pedestals and e is a T-piece made up of poorly constituted clay. It, too, has a cylindrical cross-section (Courtesy, Colchester Museum, Box label: "Sawdons Marsh Peldon, CAG No. 106, 1986.39.B2").

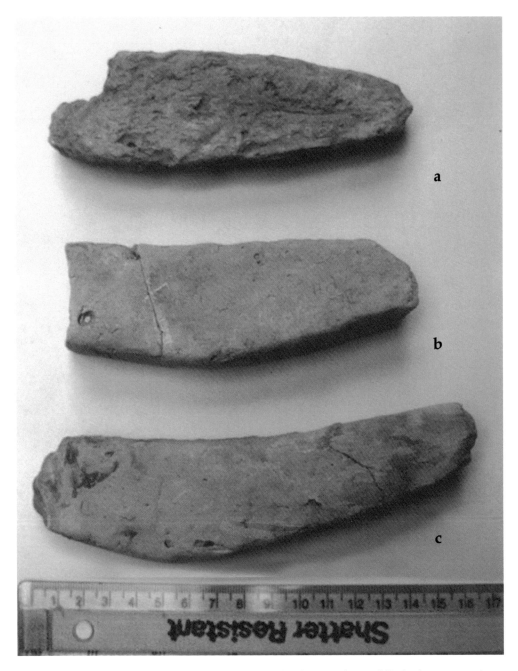

Figure 88. Firebar fragments from Langenhoe III (RH89). These specimens differ in shape suggesting they were not made by the same hands. Letters a and b have a trapezoidal cross-section while c has a rectangular cross-section (Courtesy, Colchester Museum, Box label: "CAG 89, Langenhoe III, (Pot hole below, RH & Level V, which is top of PH)").

because pedestals are not found in their context of usage at Tollesbury, but it is an important question to keep in mind. If in future investigations it turns out that the different forms were used contemporaneously, then it is more than likely different people made them. Admittedly, a person does not have to make things exactly the same each time, but as they often do, the Tollesbury excavations certainly raise some interesting issues (Figures 87 and 88).

De Brisay, Kay
The Basic Briquetage of Salt-making: A Comparative Analysis.
Colchester Archaeological Group Bulletin **24:29-39, 1981**

This article is the culmination of De Brisay's intensive research on Essex Red Hills briquetage. In it she offers both a summary description of the briquetage, as well as an interpretation as to how all the equipment might have functioned. As might be expected, most of her data come from the three excavation projects that she personally directed—Osea Road, Peldon, and Tollesbury—but for comparative information she draws liberally from briquetage sites located elsewhere in England, Poland, France, Germany, Africa, and Japan. It is a lavishly illustrated report that contains many very useful drawings. It is clear from this study that De Brisay believes the firebar to be at the heart of Essex salt production, whether supported by pedestals or hearth walls. She again emphasizes that firebars tend to be well made and untempered, whereas pedestals are of cruder construction and tempered with grains. Although there are evident distinctions between the distributions of firebars and pedestals at sites, De Brisay has finally come to accept that they are common occurrences at the same sites. The only exception is at Peldon where firebars are far more frequently recovered than pedestals. Augets, on the other hand, although common on many European sites, are almost nonexistent in this part of England. To me this suggests that salt had not yet been elevated to a currency because there was no attempt to establish a standard size container for distribution.

Having now summarized much of the early literature on the Essex Red Hills wherein the briquetage objects and their contexts have been examined, let us now turn to what this all means. We are still missing many parts of the puzzle for understanding salt making in Essex, but I do believe there is enough out there to formulate a new model that accounts for the bulk of the data.

PART III
The Red Hills Explained:
A New Model of Salt-Making

*Francis Reader, of the Red Hills Exploration
Committee, writing to a friend in 1910, said
"The indefinite matter of all these scraps makes
it necessary that the whole collection should
be gone through periodically, as I feel extended
acquaintance gradually reveals new points."*

—De Brisay 1975:5

mmediately upon returning from England I typed up my Fieldbook entry for May 27, 2005.[30] The plan was to make this an addendum to my travelogue, which indeed it was when I distributed a photocopy version of my journey in 2005. Over the ensuing months I proceeded to receive many of the publications listed in the Fawn et al. 1990 volume and upon reading those documents my preliminary model as to how salt might have been made in Essex prior to the introduction of metal containers was modified to some extent. What follows is my current thinking as to how Essex Red Hills salt manufacture occurred. Although there had to have been considerable variation of the process through time and space along the Essex landscape, the numerous consistencies in the assemblages suggest a certain degree of uniformity. The model I present here builds upon but differs significantly from that developed by DeBrisay in her important research. I do not pretend it is the final word on the subject, but it does at least account for all of the artifacts produced and, most importantly, the model is testable.

We now have a pretty good idea of the essential tools and features involved in prehistoric salt manufacture in Essex, as represented in its Red Hills. The principal archaeological features are evaporation tanks, hearths, and piles of briquetage, and the main artifact types are firebars, pedestals, troughs, wedges, pinch props, and hearth wall sections. The following issues must also be kept in mind in coming to terms with the process.

- In all probability, prehistoric salt making in Essex was a family-based seasonal industry, with the actual production of salt having occurred in the summer.
- Although they have not yet been found, the locations of salt-makers' homes were probably some distance from salt-production sites.
- Travel from home to salt-production sites would have primarily involved walking. Carts may have been used to some extent, but they would not have been able to get close to many of the Red Hills.
- Because of the location of the salt-production sites in the intertidal zone, fuel would have been limited. Therefore, it would have to have been brought to the sites.
- Evaporation tanks occur in sets, with three in a row being most common (see Figures 83 and 84).

---

[30]   GCS England Essex, pp. 66-88.

- Briquetage, the fired clay based artifacts involved in salt production, which include pottery containers, almost always occur in a broken condition.
- Firebars tend to be nicely made and seldom have temper, suggesting that they were not intended for intense heat.
- Firebars are almost always broken, with only end pieces, middle sections, or combined middle section/end pieces having been recovered (see Figures 16, 71, and 88).
- Firebars rarely have green glaze on them, whereas pedestals often do (see Figure 87).
- Pedestals (see Figures 73-75, 86, and 87) tend to be reduced, the result of either being made or used in a closed hearth, whereas firebars are highly oxidized.
- No firebar or pedestal has ever been found in the place where it was actually used, although slots in hearth walls and sockets in clay floors do provide clues as to their placement (see Figure 63).
- Pedestals often are tempered with grain or with substances that are not found locally at the Red Hills where they are recovered (see Figure 86). The addition of temper is designed to keep clay objects from exploding under intense heat.
- Pinch props seem to have been universally made out of the local London blue clay that is found beneath the Red Hill deposits.
- We now know from a complete pedestal found at Osea Road that the T-piece is but the top of a pedestal (see Figure 74d). These tops do not seem to have any beneficial means of supporting troughs or firebars. The tops are smaller than the bases, which "mushroom out" (see Figure 75).
- No complete trough has ever been found, but because some large fragments of the end, side, and base of these vessels have been joined, the basic shapes of these vessels are understood (see Figures 77, 78, 84, and 85).
- Most troughs probably would have been too heavy to carry a great distance, so some degree of construction at the salt production site seems reasonable.
- Briquetage has occasionally been found at interior sites distant from any source of salt.
- Augets have been found in large numbers on the continent during and after the Late Bronze Age (see Figure 81), but thus far there is only minimal evidence for them in Essex.

We know that the Red Hills are suitable locales for the production of salt, as they are adjacent to where tidal waters would have deposited brine into evaporating tanks (see Figures 83 and 84). It is logical that hearths would have been constructed in proximity to these tanks. The obvious lining for the walls of the hearths would be the abundant underlying London Clay. When trenches were dug, the clay walls were already "pre-made", but if ovens were to be closed to control the intensity and direction of heat, a superstructure of wattle and daub would have to be created. Here, too, the local London Clay, perhaps mixed with some silt or sand from the alluvium, would work fine.

Hearths are features that were designed on-site, but the rest of the salt-making equipment could easily have been made elsewhere. Other than Jones (1977), however, very few scholars have given this notion serious consideration with regard to the Essex Red Hills. Seeing that fuel would have run out fairly quickly along the tidal zones, it makes little sense to make anything other than

Figure 89. Two views of the same pedestal fragment from Goldhanger X (RH169). The hole in its center suggests that the clay was rolled on a cylindrical wooden object that disintegrated when the pedestal was fired (Courtesy Colchester Museum, Box label: No. 196, "Red Hills, Briquetage, Goldhanger X." Bag Label: "PSAL 22, Fig. 13.1, Fig. 14.2").

Figure 90. Wedge from Langenhoe III (RH89). The top left surface of this object is flattened and the right side near the top exhibits pushed up clay. The bottom portion is broken (Courtesy, Colchester Museum, Box label: "CAG No. 89, 1986.37.B3" and "Red Hills Langenhoe III Briquetage." Bag Label: "Langenhoe III 4").

salt at these sites if there are other solutions available. Just because pottery artifacts end up in the Red Hills, in broken form, one should not necessarily assume they were made there. The fact that the temper used in briquetage on any one site varies so much would seem to suggest they were indeed brought from distant sites. Moreover, it really does not make sense that the salt makers would have used the short summer season to roll out clay for pedestals or firebars at that time (Figure 89). It also does not seem logical that they would have hauled out temper material to add to the clay so that the pedestals upon firing would hold their shape. To me it makes far more sense that pedestals, firebars, and perhaps the wedges (Figure 90) too, would have been made at or near the comfort of their homes during the cooler months of the year. They could have easily been fashioned along with other vessels in standard pottery kilns. If this actually were done, it would not be unusual occasionally to find standard briquetage at interior sites, perhaps made by the same people who would eventually head off to the marsh to make salt during warm weather.

If we do assume that the bulk of salt-making pottery was made during the off-season in proximity to habitations, we next have to look at transportation. Just how were these objects carried to the salt-production sites? Because firebars must have been cut out of large slabs of clay into fairly standard "cookie cutter" shapes, once they were produced they could be stacked, placed in baskets, and lugged to the intertidal zone. Troughs could be handled similarly if the component parts were made in long pieces and subsequently joined to-

Figure 91. Artistic rendering of how pedestals might have been carried to the intertidal zone. Contained in the basket are wall sections of troughs that will be assembled on site. A tumpline is attached to the forehead to provide support while carrying the basket (Drawing by Jessie Foster; see also Brown 2010:Fig. 6).

gether on site. Pedestals would have been more of a problem. Because of their unusual shape, they are not easy to carry. It is possible that they could have been arranged in heaps within a cart and hauled by horse or oxen, but again, it should be stressed that the Red Hills tend to be in locations that are not easily traversed by cart. There must always have been some "over-the-back" carrying involved, and, with this in mind, this is where the T shape would have come in rather handy. A thin cord of fibrous material or leather could have been fastened to the end of the T and drawn tight. If similar cords were attached to a dozen or more pedestals, they could have easily been pulled together close to the handles to form a thick rope. With this arrangement, the cluster could be slung over a shoulder. As the salter headed off to the marsh, he would have looked as if he was carrying a large pottery cauliflower (Figure 91).

Once on site the cords would have become very tight from the weight of the pedestals, especially if they had become damp on the march. The last thing the salter would have wished to do is spend valuable daylight hours untying cords from pedestals, so I offer here another solution. It is important to remember that investigators have argued the T shape really makes no sense in support terms (Fawn et al. 1990:26). Because all that really is needed is a point of contact between pedestals and troughs, perhaps the tops of the pedestals were simply (and purposefully) broken off at the site. As the T-shaped handles had already served their purpose in transporting the pedestals, they were no longer necessary and, thus, would have merely been discarded on site. The important point in this model is that the T shape itself is not a desirable element in supporting troughs, so merely cutting the cords to preserve original pedestal shape was not warranted. If this model does prove to be a closer approximation of reality, one should expect to find a place or places on Red Hill sites where T-shaped ends occur in some frequency. These locations would have been where the worker sat to wipe his or her brow and hack away at the pedestal tops. Once that was done the bottom two-thirds or so of the pedestals would have been left to arrange in hearths. But before proceeding to just how they might have been arranged, let us next consider another prime briquetage form, the firebar.

Most students of the Essex Red Hills have observed that firebars are fairly well made objects. They tend to be of even thickness, suggesting that they were made in "cookie cutter" fashion from a large slab of clay. I do not mean to imply that an actual standard-sized mold was used, as there is considerable variation in both the size and shape of firebars, but I suspect that the clay slab would have been used efficiently. There was probably little wastage of clay as the shapes were cut out with a knife.

The standard form of a firebar is a triangle (Figure 92d), but the trapezoid shape also occurs to some extent. Most of the firebars consist of finely consolidated clays with little or no temper, which suggests that they were not intended to bear the same intensity of heat as the pedestals. The manufacturer must have realized that firebars would have had little hope for survival if they were subjected to direct heat. The fact that they are almost all highly oxidized throughout, would suggest that in their last firing (but not necessarily their use), they were surrounded by flames in an open fire and with lots of oxygen available. But when they were used in the salt production process, it is probable that they were placed some distance away from the actual fire.

It is well to remember that firebars are almost inevitably broken. Contrary to Fawn et al. (1990:26), however, I believe that they broke while in use. But just

Figure 92. Fragments of firebars from Langenhoe III (RH89). They possess the usual Essex Red Hill triangular firebar form with d being slightly concave at its widest part. These objects also lack temper, which is a general characteristic of the tool (Courtesy, Colchester Museum, Box label: "CAG No. 89, 1986.37.B3" and "Red Hills Langenhoe III Briquetage." Bag Unlabeled).

how exactly were they used? Generally the thought has been that they rested on pedestals with the apex down, the troughs then having being placed on the flat surface of the firebars. This would necessitate packing pieces of clay between the firebars and pedestals to keep the complex from toppling (Fawn et al. 1990:21). These would be arranged in sets of four pedestals and two firebars per trough, as depicted by DeBrisay (see Figure 84). It has also been thought that for sites that lack pedestals, but do have firebars, perhaps the latter were used within closed hearths by being pushed into the walls of trenches. It is thought that such an arrangement might explain just why firebars are seldom found whole (either one or both ends are generally missing). However, if that happened so frequently to produce almost constant destruction of firebars, it seems like a very poor arrangement indeed.

As so often happens when deliberating upon a problem, sometimes one receives stimulus in unexpected situations.[31] Just by chance, while sitting in Broman's Farm B&B consuming my morning repast, I happened to glance at the hearth lintel, which is in effect an extremely large firebar (see Figure 13). Although there are obvious differences in size and substance, as the lintel is an enormous structural element of good solid English oak while the firebar is small and made of friable clay, the functions of the two objects of identical shape appear to be the same. More to the point, the apex of the lintel faces upwards, which is an appropriate orientation to handle great weight coming down from above. Without the extra width in its middle, the lintel probably would have snapped centuries ago and descended on to the hearth. The same upward facing beams of firebar shape are regularly seen in English architecture, as I observed frequently in later trips through the land, so the orientation of the Broman's Farm hearth lintel really is not all that unique. Fawn et al. (1990:26) did consider the possibility of firebars having been used with their points in an upward direction, but they thought these objects would serve best with this orientation if the apices were the point of contact with the vessels. In that way, they argued, the vessels would receive better access to the heat. Such an arrangement has also been proposed to account for a large notched firebar

---

[31] "New knowledge very often has its origin in some quite unexpected observation or chance occurrence arising during an investigation. The importance of this factor in discovery should be fully appreciated and research workers ought deliberately to exploit it. Opportunities come more frequently to active bench workers and people who dabble in novel procedures. Interpreting the clue and realising [sic] its possible significance requires knowledge without fixed ideas, imagination, scientific taste, and a habit of contemplating all unexplained observations (Beveridge 1950:55)."

Figure 93. This reconstruction of salt boiling at the Roman works in, Cheshire County, is based on a large notched firebar that was recovered from a salt-working site off King Street in 1960. It would have required wedges to keep the trough horizontal if used in this manner (after Strickland 2001:Fig. 61).

found in association with a Roman saltworks at Middlewich in Cheshire, but if this were the actual orientation for firebars, the large troughs would have required wedge supports (Figure 93). Considering the height-width ratio of the Essex Red Hills firebars, however, these wedges would have had to be quite thick to serve this purpose. Those found in the Red Hills range between 1.5 and 3.0 cm (Fawn et al. 1990:13) and would not have been very effective unless they were stacked. Moreover, such an arrangement does not explain why the ends of firebars would so often be broken. Fawn et al. 1990 suggested that the cropping of the ends of firebars may actually have been intentional,[32] but I believe there might be another solution to the problem.

One will notice in the fireplace lintel at Broman's Farm that the ends are symmetrically notched (see Figure 64). The implication is that the builder knew exactly where the sides of the hearth would be and could measure the distance

---

[32] "The purpose may have been to obtain a required length, perhaps to match the width of a hearth or to fit the size of drying floor tiles. An incidental advantage would be that the weakest parts of the bars, the ends, would be eliminated and the remainder, although shorter, would be a stronger beam (Fawn et al. 1990:26)."

on the oak beam for the positioning of notching. Notches surely would give the beam far greater stability, as they would also for firebars, but the salt-makers would have to make sure that the area to be spanned would always be the same. Although the Middlewich firebar referred to above does indeed have a notch on each end, I have never seen notches on Essex firebars, so perhaps efficiency was more important than looks in this very messy industry. If that was the case, the salter would have focused more on placing pedestals or digging trenches until the lengths were "about right," meaning that they were within a certain range. As long as there was an adequate number of firebars fitting within a certain range, then the salter could select which firebars would work best to span the trench.

Be that as it may, we are still faced with the puzzle as to just how firebars might have worked in the salt making operation. If the firebars did face up, as with the lintel, then that implies force would have been coming down on each firebar from the top on two opposing sides. The firebars that I examined at the Colchester Museum that were complete enough to estimate dimensions had original lengths of 21.5 cm, 22 cm, 27 cm, 29.0 cm, 30.2 cm, and 33 cm; an average of 27.1 cm. If troughs were set on either side, the width for each vessel would have to be about half the overall length of the firebar, or around 13.6 cm. This is far too small a size for vessels recovered from the various Red Hill sites (Fawn et al. 1990:11). Plus, if brine-filled troughs were to be put on each side of the firebar, the weight could pose a major problem for the firebars and the sides of the trench might collapse.

Strength would increase if the firebars are positioned closer together, so it is worth examining what data we possess on that subject. Although not many walls with sockets have been found, some fortunately do exist. Fawn et al. (1990:23, Fig. 18) illustrate a couple of them from Goldhanger X, Site RH 169, but in the case of one of the specimens my reexamination of the object revealed that it had been depicted upside down (Figure 94). The cut section, which presumably is the rim, is shown at the bottom of their photo. Plus, as I discussed earlier, if the Goldhanger socket actually held a firebar end, it did so at an unusual angle. One very valuable bit of information from this object, however, is the appearance of another socket impression only 4.5 cm distant from the complete socket. This would suggest that two firebars had been put close together, thus strengthening the structure. In short, there must have been a rather solid pavement with long slits in between the firebars for the flow of gases.

By one of those few happy coincidences, on the last day of my sojourn in Essex I happened to go on a fieldtrip with Martin and Ruth Dence, proprietors

Figure 94. Thick section of a hearth or trench wall from Goldhanger X (RH169). It has two slots for the receipt of firebars or wedges. The bottom photo shows how a firebar correctly inserts into the slot. Note that it only fits if the point is up (Courtesy, Colchester Museum, Trench section Box label: No. 204, "Red Hills, Goldhanger, X 1906, Frags of Tanks." Bag Label: "RH 169, Goldhanger, F/B 8WL [or SWL?]. Firebar from Box Labeled: "Red Hills, Goldhanger, X 1906, Firebars").

of Broman's Farm, and Tess Sunnucks to a site on Bower Hall Farm, Mersea Island (see pp. 66-70). This is a "wet" site, meaning that it is located beyond the seawall. It is listed as site RH 86 in the Fawn et al. volume (1990:Map 2, pp. 68-69) and has quite a good pedigree. It was excavated in 1892[33] and is actually illustrated on both the front and the back covers of the Fawn et al. volume.[34] The nearby Maydays Farm sites are also well known in the literature.[35] According to the abbreviated report on the Bower Hall Farm site (Fawn et al. 1990:68-69), a 2-foot-by- 6-inch-wide trench extended to the west from the extreme edge of the hill. Stratification was not observed, but solid clay occurred beneath the alluvium. A large assortment of briquetage has been retrieved from the site over the years, including hearth wall slabs, vessel walls, pedestal T-pieces, stems, and base pieces (both mushroom and square), as well as firebar fragments. Early Roman pottery is also reported from the site. In our survey we picked up two potshards, and a piece of the hearth wall that, most remarkably, has two sockets in it (see Figure 63). They are close-spaced, as with the sherd from Goldhanger RH 169. The distance between the two sockets in the Bower Hall Farm sherd is 2.1 cm, whereas the Goldhanger sockets are spaced 4.5 cm apart. Clearly the close-spaced arrangement of the firebars is supported by this new find. What still is puzzling, however, is the discrepancy between the width of the troughs and the short length of the average firebar from end to apex, but this is only a puzzle if troughs were the actual items that were supported by firebars. Most scholars have assumed that to be the case, but it should be emphasized that there is no direct evidence for this relationship. We know that damp salt eventually had to be removed from the large troughs and placed into other containers, so why could the latter not have been baskets? Drawing from personal experiences observing salt production at the Chongtan Village in Zigong, China (Brown 2010:339; Falkenhausen and Brown 1999, 2006:67-71; Flad 2004:116-119, Fig. 2.4; 2011:41-43), it is probable that any salt put into baskets would have required further drying to remove excess liquid (Figure 95). If so, this was best done in the vicinity of the hearth so that advantage could be taken of available heat at a somewhat diminished temperature. What I suggest is that the firebars were used to support numerous flat-bottomed baskets laden

---

[33] 1888 according to Fawn et al. (1990:56).

[34] The pen and ink drawing on the back cover is an 1896 sketch by Henry Cole. The Bower Hall Farm site is probably the same as site IX (or X?) on Reader's 1910 map, which is reproduced in Fawn et al. (1990:Fig. 2). Other references to the site are included in Stopes (1887:103), Cole 1906:173, Victoria County History 1963:157 [Powell 1963], and Rodwell 1979 (his site 53).

[35] The Maydays Farm sites are listed as RH 74 and RH75 (Evans 1982:17; Fawn et al. 1990:56).

Figure 95. Scene at the Chongtan Village in Zigong, China, where traditional techniques are used to make salt in 1999. Note the large mats that are wrapped into cylinders and placed on strong shallow baskets. Beneath the line of baskets is a hidden flue that emits warm air, thus helping to dry the salt.

with damp salt, and arranged so that they covered both sides of the firebars in long linear rows. This would be most effective if the firebars were set into a clay-lined wall of a flue that emerged from the main hearth.

These baskets would not really have to be that large; in fact, they should be of such a weight that a man would be able to carry several over each shoulder, perhaps using the same cords that originally transported pedestals to the site, if that was how it was done. I will return to that momentarily, but first let us consider how the broken firebars relate to this model. If the firebars were used in the fashion that I have suggested, they would not have been subjected to intense heat and could have served their purpose for many days, if not weeks. But eventually all things do complete their life cycle and will break. I believe whole ones are not found simply because they continued to be used until they broke. Because the weakest part of the firebar would have been that portion closest to but just outside the socket, we inevitably find ends, mid-sections, or a combination of one end and a mid-section (Figure 96).

Now let us return to the pedestals and their function in the salt-making process. If firebars are removed from the formula of evaporating brine to make

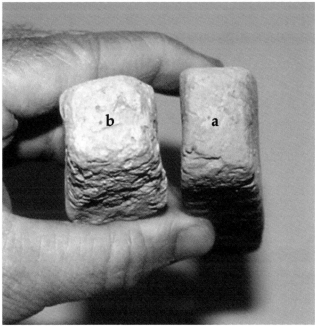

Figure 96. Two broken firebars from Sawdons Marsh, Peldon IX (RH106). Both have finished ends, one a square and the other a rectangle (Courtesy, Colchester Museum, Box label: "Sawdons Marsh Peldon Briq., CAG No. 106, 1986.39.B1." Bag Unlabeled).

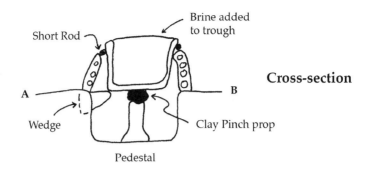

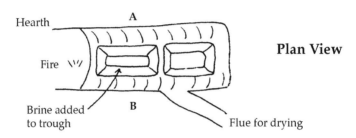

Figure 97. Schematic drawings from the author's fieldnotes of a hypothesized hearth used to produce salt. The troughs are sealed in place by wattling and thin clay rods (after Brown 2010:Fig. 4).

salt, we end up with large troughs, pedestals, wedges, and clay-lined hearths. The hearths seem to have been closed, but just how closed were they? Perhaps the troughs themselves formed a part of the "walls," the pedestals having been set randomly along the base of the hearth (Figure 97).[36] Taking small rods of clay and pushing them between the outer wall of the hearth and the troughs could make a better seal.[37]

As suggested in Fawn et al. (1990:21), the main consideration for balance is that each vessel touches three pedestals. Two would provide only precarious stability, whereas three would serve as a very solid tripod arrangement for the

---

[36] This reconstruction works most effectively with vessels of rectangular shape, which is the typical shape of the supposed evaporating pans (Fawn et al. 1990:11). There would be far too much leakage of gasses with circular vessels, which are quite prevalent on the Red Hill sites, but it is certainly possible that the spaces in between the vessels could have been filled with clay, as has been observed in Niger (Gouletquer 1975).

[37] "Crudely hand-fashioned rods of fired clay have been found…The largest is about 18 cm long and 3 cm in diameter. The ends bear the impressions of other rounded objects, the nature of which is not known. Reader referred to them as 'handles', but this use appears doubtful (Fawn et al. 1990:14, Fig. 15)."

troughs. To improve balance small clumps of clay could have been set on top of the now "T-less" pedestals, with each trough being pushed down on to the clay to establish both a level and a balance. These clay clumps may be what has been described in the literature as "pinch props":

> These odd-shaped pieces of briquetage are also comparatively scarce, but many may not have been recognized and collected. No one piece is like another, their only common features being that each has a flat base and at least one other facet suggesting contact with two surfaces, one flat and one angular (Fig. 14).
>
> They contain no organic tempering and appear to be lumps of raw clay which were pressed into gaps between other briquetage components and became fired in the course of the process.
>
> —Fawn et al. 1990:13

It is worth noting that a similar complex of cylinders and pinch prop-like equipment has been found along the coast of Belize in Mesoamerica. The cylinders lack flared bases or t-shaped tops, however. Instead, they are of equal diameter throughout. The archaeologists who have worked on these sites, many of which are now submerged, believe that the cylinders represent pedestals, which supported a series of constricted jars bearing flared rims (Mackinnon and Kepecs 1989; McKillop 1995; 2002:62-69,112-114; Valdez and Mock 1991). It is believed the cylinders were used in sets of three to hold each respective jar in place. Each cylinder was first pushed into a clump of clay and set in the floor. Consequently, the clumps would appear as sockets once they were separated from the cylinders. We know from those clumps that remained connected to the cylinders that they were set an angle, and presumably slanted inwards. The top of each of the three cylinders was then capped with another lump of clay, again forming a socket piece, and the vessel was pressed down on to the pedestals to hold it securely in place. It is thought that the other lumps of clay served as spacers between the vessels. Perhaps of significance is the observation that these spacers and sockets are far more friable than the cylinders because they would not have baked as well in the salt-making process.

From the various reconstruction illustrations that are offered in the above studies an open fire seems to be the general interpretation. I suppose this is because hearths and trenches have not yet been found, but surely an enclosed oven would have been far more fuel-efficient. From my reading of the various Belize salt studies, the cylinders are thought to have been made on-site but, again, it seems more logical to me that the salt-makers would have fashioned cylinders inland where more fuel was available and when they had ample time. Why spend time on the coast making equipment that you could have created beforehand? I believe that the numerous instances of cylinders having been found on sites that lack sockets and spacers are supportive of the inland workshop hypothesis (Mackinnon and Kepecs 1989:525; 1991:529).

But let us return to those large troughs from the Essex Red Hills to examine how they were made? Once again, it does not seem reasonable to me that the producers would have used valuable time on site to make them. It is important to remember that although numerous examples of corners and other bends have been found, no where has a complete or near complete trough been recovered. The one from the Peldon Red Hill (RH 117) comes closest to being whole (Fawn et al. 1990:Fig. 7), but even this vessel is but a corner of one large vessel. I think it is significant that these troughs, which make up perhaps more than 90% of the briquetage on Red Hills,[38] generally tend to be flat slab fragments.

> *Many other joined fragments indicate that vessels with vertical as well as splayed sides were used. Most of the Type A vessels from the north-east seem to have been rectangular or sub-rectangular. As far as can be judged from the incomplete examples found, the method of fabrication was variable. Some appear to have been made from two sides, two ends and a base joined together. Some may have been formed from a long length of clay bent and joined to form the four walls, with the base then being added. Others have obviously been made by bending a slab of clay into a U form to form the base and sides and then adding two more slabs to form the ends.*
>
> —Fawn et al. 1990:11

The impression one gets from the above quote is that these vessels may have started off as fragments, essentially prefabricated tiles of varying shapes that were spliced together on site. This is certainly the case with a number of the trough shards that I examined at the Colchester Museum, whose cross-sections showed clear evidence of multiple layers of clay at the joints (Figures 98–99). As with the pedestals and firebars, it would have been far more expeditious to fashion the components of the troughs off site where there was abundant fuel and ample time. Transporting them to the site would have been easier if they were flat pieces that could be stacked and, later, joined together

---

[38]   Excluding hearth wall debris.

Figure 98. Cross-section of a trough sherd from Goldhanger X (RH169). It can clearly be seen that the vessel corner consists of two separate slabs joined at a right angle (Courtesy, Colchester Museum, Box label: No. 113, "Red Hills, Goldhanger, X Troughs").

Figure 99. One hearth wall fragment (a) and three trough shards from Langenhoe III (RH89). The interior of each of the troughs is to the right. The lower photo, which is an enlargement of sherd d, reveals that a second layer of clay was added at the joint (Courtesy, Colchester Museum, Box label: "CAG 89, Langenhoe III, (Pot hole below, RH & Level V, which is top of PH)").

using the ubiquitous London Clay (Figures 91 and 100). An initial on-site firing would have baked the joints enough to hold up for the operation. The pouring in of brine would have occurred only after the vessel had sufficient time to cool down, which might be several days later. If this actually happened, it certainly would explain the absence of complete or even near-complete troughs on Red Hill sites. The weakest points on these vessels would always have been the most recent joints, and when they eventually cracked, the whole lot would simply be shoveled out and added as a "tip" to the pile of rapidly accumulating briquetage nearby. The

Figure 100. Stage 1 of the new model of Essex Red Hills salt making. Pedestals and firebars are shown being made on a flat surface at a habitation. Trough sections that were manufactured earlier are stacked and placed in a large basket (Drawing by Jessie Foster; see also Brown 2010:Fig. 5).

cleaned-out hearth would still have within it many highly reduced pedestals that were heavily damaged, but still useful if they stood up to a reasonable height. The lifespan of a hearth would have been much longer than the troughs or the hearth walls, and firebars would have had the longest lifespan of all.

When the day was done, the ancient salt-makers would have gathered together their handful of baskets laden with dried salt. Somewhat larger baskets may have been used earlier in the day to lug out to the site wall sections of troughs and perhaps even a few firebars. Not many of the latter would have been needed, however; only a few replacements. The small baskets full of salt could have easily been carried using the same cords that were initially tied to the T-pieces of pedestals. At some later time the salters would need to bring out another "cauliflower of pedestals" (see Figure 91) to replenish the supply, but this next trip would not involve the actual making of salt. The next time, perhaps in a few days, the used troughs and broken walls of the hearth would be hammered away and cleaned out. A new webbing of wattle, in a basic U-shaped form, would then be erected over the hearth, and perhaps that too could have been more easily fashioned back at the farm. This framework would have been relatively easy to carry and set up, gaining substantial weight only when the wattling was set in place and packed with clay from the underlying London Clay substratum. This newly crafted hearth would have to dry for a while, perhaps for several weeks, before it could be used to produce salt, and then the process would start anew.

At this point in time, it is not possible to tell whether the process of Essex Red Hill salt making that has been presented here is correct. However, the model does fit reasonably well with the majority of the data, but not all. If there is one thing the various studies of the Red Hills have demonstrated over the years, the early salters of southeast England were a creative lot. They ingeniously fashioned their work areas in ways that would produce ample salt in what was presumably the most economical means possible.[39] Fuel had to be gotten to the site, as did the implements necessary to extract salt from the brine, and there was always someone who was going to try a slightly different way to make things more efficient. Tradition is the binding element for behavior, but innovation is what makes people such a delight to study.

---

[39] I am very aware that people often do not do that which is "obviously" most logical in economic terms. There are numerous reasons why people of the past and present behave in manners that defy logic. Nevertheless, archaeologists must follow first the premise that economy guides action and when that does not work, which is often the case, other explanations must be sought.

Figure 101. Stage 2 of the new model of Essex Red Hills salt making. There is lots of activity in this scene. The young boy in the top left breaks the tops off pedestals that were just carried to the site. The girl in the lower left applies lumps of malleable clay to the broken stems of the pedestals. The man in the middle places the pedestals in a seemingly random fashion, but each trough will eventually fit snugly on at least three of them. In the upper right a woman assembles trough sections using the local London Clay to form large vessels (Drawing by Jessie Foster; see also Brown 2010:Fig. 7).

If this model of Red Hills salt production is viable, I would expect the following characteristics of the ideal site: In addition to the usual evaporating tanks, filled by tidal waters (in sets of at least three, as seen from past excavations), there should be an ample-sized hearth that runs linearly for distances of at least two or three times its width (Figure 101). In the initial stages of Red Hill formation, these hearths should have been dug into the London Clay, the result being a trench. The bottom of the trench should either have impressions of the flared bases of pedestals or, if one is so lucky to find a production site that was merely abandoned, the pedestals should still be in place. Clay pinch props should also be expected in the trench, and perhaps short clay rods too. Ample amounts of clay hearth walls bearing wattling impressions should also occur. The pedestals should be gray to black in color, the result of having been continually baked in a closed hearth with little oxygen. They should all be fragmentary, with the T-shaped tops missing. These tops should be found in

Figure 102. Stage 3 of the new model of Essex Red Hills salt making. The salt-making process is about to begin in this reconstruction. The fire has been lit at one end of the trench and brine is being shifted from one evaporation pit to the next in order to enrich it. The solution will be poured into the troughs and, as salt eventually forms, the moist crystals will be placed in baskets to be dried on top of the firebars. These objects are arranged close together and bridge a secondary flue, which is distant from the fire. The scene is hypothetical but does account for the majority of items found on Essex Red Hill sites (Drawing by Jessie Foster; see also Brown 2010:Fig. 8).

a pile close by and it is expected that those found in the same location should have the same temper. Different piles could possibly have different tempers, depending on the preference of the person(s) who made them. Within the trench there could be a mixture of pedestals bearing different tempers, because pedestals would have been reused if they were still serviceable. These pedestals should also have plenty of glaze drippings on them from vaporized salt. Also within the trench, if one should ever be found that was simply abandoned, there should be large fragments of troughs. Most of the trough shards, however, would have ended up in the tips of the growing Red Hill deposit because the hearths were repetitively restored. Assuming these troughs were prefabricated, only large slabs will be found, or mostly shards with a slight bend in their walls. This is because the troughs would have broken easiest at joints while in use.

The items that probably had the longest life were firebars, largely due to them having been used some distance from the hearth on top of associated flues.[40] If firebars really were utilized in the manner that has been proposed here, they would be oxidized entirely from one end to the other. If ever any of these firebars are found in place, I predict that they will either be set on or just below the lip of the trench, they will be close together, and their apices will face up (Figure 102). The clay walls in these flues should have a line of slots in them, all spaced 2 to 5 cm apart to permit gases to flow between the firebars. Slots should also be found in hearth walls periodically and these, I believe, will have wedges in them, all reduced because they were within the closed oven. Thus, although wedges had a similar function as the firebars, their context of usage was different I believe. It is unlikely that an entire firebar will be found though, because as long as it remained whole it would have been reused. Instead, only end pieces, middle sections, or a single end/mid-section combination will occur.

Most of the above "predictions" already match well with the known archaeological record, but there is still much digging that is needed at Red Hill sites. Until an abandoned hearth is found, one that has preserved the last salt-making event squarely contained within its walls, the archaeologists' endeavors will remain one of piecing together the process from the fragments. A hundred years ago Francis Reader made an appeal for two main areas of continued study—features and museum collections. His wisdom holds as much value today as it did a century ago when he led the Red Hills Exploration Committee and its profound contributions to the study of salt.

> *It is sufficient perhaps to point out the characteristic features denoting the various sites and leave the question of chronology until more is definitely known of this subject. A great advance has been made in this direction during the last few years, and further study of the associated groups from Essex in the Colchester Museum and elsewhere, in conjunction with other discoveries that may occur in the future, will probably do much to throw light on this matter. Such variations as I have endeavored to point out may then be shown to have more significance.*
>
> —Reader 1908b:194

---

[40]   The best examples of flues, often arranged in pairs, can be seen at RH176, the Goldhanger VIII site (Reader 1910a:Figs. 4-5).

References Cited

Atkinson, J. C.
1880   Some Further Notes on the Salting Mounds of Essex. *The Archaeological Journal* 37:196-199.

Bacon, Francis
1982   *Selected Writings* [Essays, Advancement of Learning, New Atlantis]. The Franklin Library, Franklin Center, Pennsylvania.

Beveridge, William Ian B.
1950   *The Art of Scientific Investigation*. Vintage Books, New York.

Biddulph, Edward, Stuart Foreman, Elizabeth Stafford, Dan Stansbie, and Rebecca Nicholson
2012   *London Gateway: Iron Age and Roman Salt Making in the Thames Estuary*. Excavation at Stanford Wharf Nature Reserve, Essex. Oxford Archaeology Monograph 18. Oxford.

Brown, Ian W.
1980   *Salt and the Eastern North American Indian: An Archaeological Study*. Lower Mississippi Survey Bulletin No. 6. Peabody Museum, Harvard University.

1999a   The Pointed Base Pottery Cup Vessel Form, a Probable Tool of Salt Production in Central China. Unpublished ms., Gulf Coast Survey, The University of Alabama, Tuscaloosa.

1999b   Studying Salt in Central China. Unpublished ms., Gulf Coast Survey, The University of Alabama, Tuscaloosa.

2006   The Pointed-Base Pottery Cup Vessel Form: A Probable Tool of Salt Production. In *Salt Archaeology in China: Ancient Salt Production and Landscape Archaeology in the Upper Yangzi Basin: Preliminary Studies. Vol. 1*, edited by Shuicheng Li and Lothar von Falkenhausen, pp. 260-285. Kexue chubanshe (Science Press), Beijing.

2010   Comparison of the Briquetage from Zhongba to Finds from the Essex Red Hills of Southeast England. In *Salt Archaeology in China: Global Comparative Perspectives. Vol. 2*, edited by Shuicheng Li and Lothar von Falkenhausen, pp. 320-345. Kexue chubanshe (Science Press), Beijing.

Clarke, Helen
1984   *The Archaeology of Medieval England*. British Museum Publications Ltd, London.

Cole, William
1906   Exploration of Some "Red Hills" in Essex, with Remarks Upon the Objects Found. *Essex Naturalist* 14 (Pt. 6):170-183.

Crawford, Osbert G. S.
1970   Archaeology in the Field. J. M. Dent Ltd, London [orig. pub. 1953].

De Brisay, Kay
1972   Preliminary Report on the Exploration of the Red Hill at Osea Road, Maldon, Essex. *Colchester Archaeological Group Bulletin* 15:23-43.

1973   A Further Report on the Excavation of the Red Hill at Osea Road, Maldon, Essex. 1972. *Colchester Archaeological Group Bulletin* 16:19-38.

1974   The Excavation of a Red Hill at Peldon, Essex: Report on the First Year. *Colchester Archaeological Group Bulletin* 17:25-42.

1975   The Red Hills of Essex. In *Salt, the Study of an Ancient Industry*, edited by K. W. De Brisay and K. A. Evans, pp. 5–11. Colchester Archaeological Group, Colchester.

1978a   The Excavation of a Red Hill at Peldon, Essex, with Notes on Some Other Sites. *The Antiquaries Journal* 58 (Pt. 1):31-60.

1978b   A Red Hill at Tollesbury, Essex: Its Background & Excavation, Report on the First Year. *Colchester Archaeological Group Bulletin* 21:5-10.

1979   The Red Hill at Tollesbury, Essex: Final Report. *Colchester Archaeological Group Bulletin* 22:2-8.

1981   The Basic Briquetage of Salt-making: A Comparative Analysis. *Colchester Archaeological Group Bulletin* 24:29-39.

De Brisay, Kay, and K.[Kath] A. Evans (eds.)
1975   *Salt, the Study of an Ancient Industry*. Colchester Archaeological Group, Colchester.

Deuel, Leo
1971   *Flights into Yesterday: the Story of Aerial Archaeology*. MacDonald and Co. Ltd, London [orig. pub. 1969].

Dence, Colin
1985   *Season to Taste*. Food Trade, Orpington, England.

Dickens, Charles
2000   *American Notes*. Könemann Verlagsgesellschaft mbH, Bonner Strafse, Köln, Germany.

Evans, Kath
1982   The Examination of the Remains of Two Small Red Hills at Maydays Farm, East Mersea. *Colchester Archaeological Group Annual Bulletin* 25:17-18.

Falkenhausen, Lothar von, and Ian W. Brown
1999   Descriptive and Analytical Notes from a Research Trip to Sichuan and the Three Gorges. Unpublished Report Submitted to the Wenner-Gren Foundation for Anthropological Research.

2006   Report on the Preliminary Field Season in 1999 (March 1-28, 1999). In *Salt Archaeology in China: Ancient Salt Production and Landscape Archaeology in the Upper Yangzi Basin: Preliminary Studies. Vol. 1*, edited by Shuicheng Li and Lothar von Falkenhausen, pp. 30-113. Kexue chubanshe (Science Press), Beijing.

Fawn, A. J., K. A. Evans, I. McMaster, and G. M. R. Davies
1990   *The Red Hills of Essex: Salt-Making in Antiquity.* Colchester Archaeological Group, Colchester.

Flad, Rowan K.
2004   *Specialized Salt Production and Changing Social Structure at the Prehistoric Site of Zhongba in the Eastern Sichuan Basin, China.* Ph.D. Dissertation, University of California, Los Angeles.

2011   *Salt Production and Social Hierarchy in Ancient China: An Archaeological Investigation of Specialization in China's Three Gorges.* Cambridge University Press, Cambridge.

Gouletquer, P. L.
1975   Niger, Country of Salt. In *Salt, the Study of an Ancient Industry,* edited by K. W. De Brisay and K. A. Evans, pp. 47–51. Colchester Archaeological Group, Colchester.

Hughes, Nigel
2000   *Maya Monuments.* Antique Collectors' Club, Woodbridge, England.

Jefferies, R. S., and P. M. Barford
1990   Gazetteer 3: Pottery from Essex Red Hills. In *The Red Hills of Essex: Salt-Making in Antiquity,* by A. J. Fawn et al., pp. 73-78. Colchester Archaeological Group, Colchester.

Jenkins, J. H. B.
1910   Remarks on Dr. Flinders Petrie's Theory. *Proceedings of the Society of Antiquaries of London,* 2nd Series 23: 90-96.

Jones, M. U.
1977   Prehistoric Salt Equipment from a Pit at Mucking, Essex. *The Antiquaries Journal* 57(Pt. 2): 317–319.

King, Jackie (editor)

1999   *Alastair Sawday's Special Places to Stay: British Bed & Breakfast, 4th ed.*
The Globe Pequot Press, Guilford, Connecticut, and Alastair
Sawday Publishing, Bristol, United Kingdom.

Kipling, Rudyard

n.d.   *American Notes.* J. H. Sears & Company, Inc., New York, New York.

Kleinmann, Dorothée

1975   The Salt Springs of the Saale Valley. In *Salt, the Study of an Ancient
Industry,* edited by K. W. De Brisay and K. A. Evans, pp. 45–46.
Colchester Archaeological Group, Colchester.

MacKinnon, J. Jefferson, and Susan M. Kepecs

1989   Prehispanic Saltmaking in Belize: New Evidence.
American Antiquity 54(3):522–533.

1991   Prehispanic Saltmaking in Belize: a Reply to Valdez and Mock and
to Marcus. *American Antiquity* 56(3):528–530.

McKillop, Heather

1995   Underwater Archaeology, Salt Production, and Coastal Maya Trade
at Stingray Lagoon, Belize. *Latin American Antiquity* 6(3):214–228.

2002   *Salt: White Gold of the Ancient Maya.* University Press of Florida,
Gainesville.

Morris, Elaine L.

1985   Prehistoric Salt Distributions: Two Case Studies from Western
Britain. *Bulletin of the Board of Celtic Studies* 32:336-379.

1994   Production and Distribution of Pottery and Salt in Iron Age
Britain: A Review. *Proceedings of the Prehistoric Society* 60:371-393.

Ottaway, Patrick

1992   *Archaeology in British Towns: From the Emperor Claudius to the
Black Death.* Routledge, London and New York.

Petrie, William Flinders

1910   Suggested Origin of the Red Hills. *Proceedings of the Society of Antiquaries of London*, 2nd Series 23: 88–90.

Powell, W. R.

1963   *The Victoria History of the County of Essex*. Vol. 3, Roman Essex. Dawson for the University of London, Institute of Historical Research, London.

Reader, Francis W.

1908a   Report of the Red Hills Exploration Committee, 1906–7. *Proceedings of the Society of Antiquaries of London*, 2nd Series 22: 165–181.

1908b   Additional Remarks on the Pottery and Briquetage Found in the Red Hills of Essex, and Similar Objects from Other Localities. *Proceedings of the Society of Antiquaries of London*, 2nd Series 22: 190–207.

1910a   Report of the Red Hills Exploration Committee 1908–9. *Proceedings of the Society of Antiquaries of London*, 2nd Series 23: 69–83.

1910b   Notes on the Briquetage Found in 1908–9. *Proceedings of the Society of Antiquaries of London*, 2nd Series 23: 86–88.

Riehm, Karl

1961   Prehistoric Salt–boiling. *Antiquity* 35(139): 181–191.

Rodwell, Warwick

1979   Iron Age and Roman Salt-winning on the Essex Coast. In *Invasion and Response*, edited by B. C. Burnham and H. B. Johnson, pp. 133-175. British Archaeological Reports No. 73.

Sealey, P[aul] R.

1995   New Light on the Salt Industry and Red Hills of Prehistoric and Roman Essex. *Essex Archaeology and History* 26:65-81.

Soudah, Gillian
1987   *The Salt Maker of Maldon*. Ian Henry Publications Ltd, Ramford, Essex.

Stevenson, Robert Louis
1997   *Travels with a Donkey in the Cevennes*. Könemann, Köln, Hungary.

2004   *An Inland Voyage and Other European Tales*. The Folio Society, London.

Smith, Reginald A.
1918   (The Essex Red Hills as Saltworks). *Proceedings of the Society of Antiquaries of London*, 2nd Series 30: 36–53.

Stopes, H.
1879   The Salting Mounds of Essex. *The Archaeological Journal* 36: 369–372.

Strickland, Tim
2001   *Roman Middlewich: A Story of Roman and Briton in Mid-Cheshire*. The Roman Middlewich Project, Middlewich.

Tessier, Michel
1975   The Protohistoric Salt Making Sites of the Pays de Retz, France. In *Salt, the Study of an Ancient Industry*, edited by K. W. De Brisay and K. A. Evans, pp. 52–56. Colchester Archaeological Group, Colchester.

Valdez, Fred Jr., and Shirley B. Mock
1991   Additional Considerations for Prehispanic Saltmaking in Belize. *American Antiquity* 56(3):520–525.

Wilmer, [Horace]
1918   (Comments on "The Essex Red Hills as Saltworks" by Reginald A. Smith). *Proceedings of the Society of Antiquaries of London*, 2nd Series 30: 53-54.

Winslow, John H., and Alfred Meyer
1983   The Perpetrator at Piltdown. *Science* 83, September, pp. 33-43.

CPSIA information can be obtained
at www.ICGtesting.com
Printed in the USA
LVIC06n0746040114
367872LV00003B/3